GREAT
WHISKEYS

Material previously published in *World Whiskey*

GREAT WHISKEYS

500 of the BEST FROM AROUND THE WORLD

EDITOR-IN-CHIEF **CHARLES MACLEAN**

Penguin Random House

2018 EDITION

DK UK & US

Editorial Assistant Rosamund Cox
Senior Editor Kate Meeker
US Editor Megan Douglass
Americanizer Michelle Melani
Senior Art Editor Glenda Fisher
Senior Jacket Creative Nicola Powling
Producer, Pre-Production Robert Dunn
Producer Igrain Roberts
Creative Technical Support Sonia Charbonnier
Managing Editor Stephanie Farrow
Managing Art Editor Christine Keilty

DK INDIA

Project Editor Arani Sinha
Assistant Editor Nonita Saha
DTP Designers Umesh Singh Rawat,
Manish Chandra Upreti
Senior DTP Designer Tarun Sharma
Pre-Production Manager Sunil Sharma
Managing Editor Soma Chowdhury

Material previously published in World Whiskey, 2009, 2016
This American Edition, 2018
First American Edition, 2011
Published in the United States by DK Publishing
345 Hudson Street, New York, New York 10014

A catalog record for this book
is available from the Library of Congress.
ISBN: 978-1-4654-7321-9

Printed and bound in China

A WORLD OF IDEAS:
SEE ALL THERE IS TO KNOW

www.dk.com

CONTENTS

INTRODUCTION

There's an old saying in Scotland: "There's no bad whisky. Just good whisky and better whisky." The whiskeys featured in this book come from all over the world. As you will see, great whiskey is now being made in South Asia, Australasia, and Europe, not just the "established" whiskey countries of Scotland, Ireland, the US, Canada, and Japan.

Whiskey is recognized as the most complex spirit on the planet. It is made from the simplest and most natural of ingredients—cereal grains, water, and yeast—yet the craft and tradition that goes into its making elevate it to the rank of "noble spirit," presenting a huge spectrum of aromas and tastes. Like people, every whiskey is different—each has its own personality. Some are big, bold, and rowdy; others delicate, elegant, and shy. Some you may not take to immediately may later become good friends. My selection has been guided by six of the world's leading whiskey writers—Dave Broom, Tom Bruce-Gardyne, Ian Buxton, Peter Mulryan, Hans Offringa, and Gavin D. Smith—and I am deeply grateful to them for writing up the individual entries.

How you choose to enjoy whiskey—with or without water or ice; with soda or lemonade; with ginger ale or cola—is a matter of personal preference. In China they like it with iced tea, in Brazil with coconut water. However "flavor" is not just about taste, it also embraces smell. Indeed, to truly appreciate the nuances of flavor in whiskey, particularly malt whisky, you should add nothing but a dash of water, and present the drink in a glass that allows you to consider its aroma to the fullest.

Secreted within this listing of world whiskeys are tours that will guide you to whiskey regions of Scotland, Ireland, the US, and Japan. No experience adds more to the enjoyment of whiskey than visiting a working distillery to savor the aromas; appreciate the skill, dedication, and time that goes into making this profound spirit; and of course, to sample a dram right at its source.

Maybe you are just setting out on this journey of discovery; perhaps you're well down the road to becoming a connoisseur. Either way, I hope this book will be a useful guide and will introduce you to some interesting flavors.

Explore and enjoy!

Charles MacLean

8PM

India

Owner: Radico Khaitan
www.radicokhaitan.com

Launched as recently as 1999, 8PM had the singular distinction of selling a million cases in its first year (it now sells 3 million). The brand owner is Radico Khaitan, based at Rampur Distillery, Uttar Pradesh. Established in 1943, it is now a gigantic unit with a capacity of over 20 million gallons (90 million liters) of alcohol a year.

The company owns other whiskey brands, including Whytehall, and it has recently formed a partnership with Diageo, the world's largest drinks conglomerate, to produce Masterstroke (see p248).

◄ 8PM CLASSIC

BLEND

Made from "a mix of quality grains," this has a core that promises "*thaath*" (boldness, opulence) and "the reach of a man to the dream world."

8PM ROYALE

BLEND

A blend of Indian spirits and mature Scotch malt whiskies.

100 PIPERS

Scotland
Owner: Chivas Brothers

Created in 1965 by Seagram, and named after an old Scots song, 100 Pipers was originally a contender in the "value" sector of the Scotch whisky market, where it was an immediate success. The blend contains malts from Allt-á-Bhainne and Braeval (distilleries that mainly supply malts for blends), and probably some Glenlivet and Longmorn as well. Seagrams developed the brand very effectively and it has continued to prosper under the new owners, Chivas Brothers (themselves owned by Pernod Ricard). It is one of the best-selling whiskies in Thailand, a dynamic market for Scotch, and is growing rapidly in many countries, especially Spain, Venezuela, Australia, and India.

100 PIPERS ▶

BLEND 40% ABV
Pale in color. A light and very mixable whisky, with a smooth yet subtly smoky taste.

ABERFELDY

Scotland
Aberfeldy, Perthshire
www.aberfeldy.com

Aberfeldy was built by John Dewar & Sons in 1898 to supply malts for the company's blends, but now also offers some single malt bottlings. Its lifelong bond with Dewar's White Label is celebrated at its impressive, fully interactive visitor center, Dewar's World of Whisky, opened in 2000. Visitors see the rudiments of malt whisky distilling, but the main emphasis is on the art of blending and the role of Tommy Dewar (1864–1930), arguably the greatest whisky baron of them all.

◀ ABERFELDY 12-YEAR-OLD
SINGLE MALT: HIGHLANDS 40% ABV
The standard expression has a clean, apple-scented nose with a medium-bodied fruity character in the mouth.

ABERFELDY 21-YEAR-OLD
SINGLE MALT: HIGHLANDS 40% ABV
Launched in 2005, this has greater depth and richness than the 12-year-old, with a sweet, heathery nose and a slight spicy catch on the finish.

ABERLOUR

Scotland
Aberlour, Banffshire
www.aberlour.com

Aberlour's extreme popularity in France makes it one of the top ten best-selling malts in the world. As part of the old Campbell Distillers, it has been owned by the French group Pernod Ricard since 1975. Its malt is used in a great number of blends, particularly in Clan Campbell, but up to half the production is bottled as a single malt in a wide range of age statements and finishes.

ABERLOUR 12-YEAR-OLD DOUBLE CASK MATURED ▶
SINGLE MALT: SPEYSIDE 40% ABV
Soft nose of cloves, nutmeg, and banana. The spicy pear and dark berry palate leads to a slightly bitter oak finish, with sherry and a wisp of smoke.

ABERLOUR A'BUNADH
SINGLE MALT: SPEYSIDE 60% ABV
A'bunadh *(a-boon-ahh)*, "the origin" in Gaelic, is a cask strength, non–chill filtered malt matured in Oloroso casks. It has a sumptuous character of fruitcake and spice.

ADNAMS

England

*Copper House Distillery, Adnams PLC,
Sole Bay Brewery, Southwold, Suffolk
www.adnams.co.uk*

Adnams Brewery has been a feature of the Suffolk town of Southwold since 1872; in 2010, a license was granted to distill on the site, and distilling equipment was subsequently installed in a redundant brewhouse building.

Adnams released its first two whiskies in 2013: Triple Grain No.2 and Single Malt No.1. Both are produced from local, East Anglian grains, with the former matured in American oak barrels and the latter in French oak casks. Adnams also distills gin, vodka, and absinthe.

◀ ADNAMS COPPER HOUSE SINGLE MALT NO.1

SINGLE MALT 43% ABV

New oak opens the nose, soon followed by vanilla, honey, and spices. Caramel, apples, and black pepper on the palate.

ALBERTA

Canada

*1521 34th Avenue Southeast,
Calgary, Alberta*
Owner: Jim Beam

Alberta Distillery was founded in Calgary in 1946 to take advantage of the immense Canadian prairies and the fine Rocky Mountain water. Rye is at the heart of many Canadian whiskies, and is predominant in Alberta. Maturing takes place in first-fill bourbon casks, or even in new white-oak casks. Other brands from Alberta include Tangle Ridge (*see p339*) and Windsor Canadian (*see p374*).

ALBERTA SPRINGS 10-YEAR-OLD ▶

CANADIAN RYE 40% ABV
A sweet aroma, with rye bread and black pepper. The taste is very sweet, even somewhat cloying, becoming charred and caramelized.

ALBERTA PREMIUM

CANADIAN RYE 40% ABV
Described as "Special Mild Canadian Rye Whisky." The aroma presents vanilla toffee, a hint of spice, light citric notes, and fruitiness. The taste is sweet above all, with stewed apples, plums, and marzipan.

13

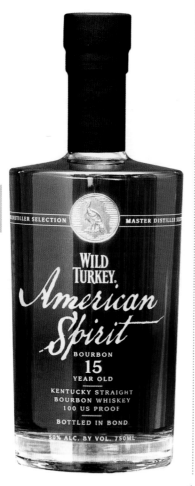

AMERICAN SPIRIT

US

Wild Turkey Distillery,
US Highway 62 East,
Lawrenceburg, Kentucky
www.wildturkeybourbon.com

American Spirit is distilled at the
Wild Turkey Distillery (*see p367*)
by Austin Nicholls & Co, and was
introduced in September 2007.
According to Eddie Russell, who
developed this expression with
his father, Master Distiller Jimmy
Russell, the name "American
Spirit" seemed to suggest itself.

◀ AMERICAN SPIRIT 15-YEAR-OLD
BOURBON 50% ABV
Richly aromatic and characterful
on the nose and silky smooth in
the mouth, with vanilla, brittle toffee,
molasses, stewed fruits, spice, and
a little mint. The finish is lengthy
and spicy, with gentle oak and
a final menthol note.

AMRUT

India
www.amrutwhisky.co.uk

In Hindu mythology, the amrut was a golden pot containing the elixir of life. This family-owned Indian company focuses on innovation, quality, and transparency: they use barley grown in the Punjabi foothills of the Himalayas, malted in Jaipur, and distilled in small batches 3,000 ft (900 m) above sea level in Bangalore, where it is matured in ex-bourbon and new oak casks and bottled without chill filtration.

AMRUT INDIAN SINGLE MALT CASK STRENGTH ▶
SINGLE MALT 61.9% ABV
Lightly fruity and cereal-like; bourbon casks introduce toffee. More woody, spicy, and malty with water. Similar in profile to a young Speyside malt.

AMRUT PEATED INDIAN SINGLE MALT
SINGLE MALT 62.78% ABV
Cereal and kippery smoke on the nose; oily, with salt and pepper. The taste is sweet and malty, with a whiff of smoke in the finish.

ANCIENT AGE

US

Buffalo Trace,
1001 Wilkinson Boulevard,
Frankfort, Kentucky
www.buffalotracedistillery.com

Ancient Age was, from 1969 to 1999, the name of what is now the Buffalo Trace Distillery (*see p66*). The brand was introduced in the 1930s shortly after the end of Prohibition, initially being distilled in Canada. After World War II, it was reformulated as a straight Kentucky-made bourbon, and went on to become one of the best-known brands produced by its proprietors.

◀ ANCIENT AGE 10-YEAR-OLD
BOURBON 40% ABV

This 10-year-old bourbon is complex and fragrant on the nose, with spices, fudge, oranges, and honey. It is medium-bodied and, after a slightly dry opening, the oily palate sweetens, developing vanilla and cocoa flavors, and a lightly charred note.

ANCNOC

Scotland
*Knockdhu Distillery, Knock,
Huntly, Aberdeenshire*
www.ancnoc.com

Named after the nearby "Black
Hill," the springs of which supply
its water, anCnoc is the core
expression of Knockdhu Distillery.

Historically significant for being
the first distillery built by the
Distillers Company Limited
(DCL), Knockdhu's new owner,
Inver House, has kept the
character of the distillery.
The traditional worm tubs for
condensing the spirit add a slightly
sulfury, meaty character to the
new make.

ANCNOC VINTAGE 2000 ▶
SINGLE MALT: SPEYSIDE 46% ABV
Toffee, vanilla, plums, spicy orange,
and chocolate on the nose. Cocoa,
vanilla, nutty sherry, nutmeg, and
black pepper on the smooth palate.

ANCNOC 12-YEAR-OLD
SINGLE MALT: SPEYSIDE 40% ABV
A relatively full-bodied Speyside
malt, with notes of lemon peel and
heather-honey on the nose, a fairly
luscious mouthfeel, and some length
on the finish.

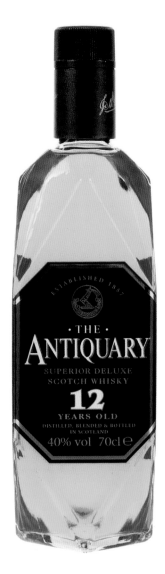

THE ANTIQUARY

Scotland

Owner: Tomatin Distillery
www.theantiquary.com

Introduced in 1857 and named after a novel by Sir Walter Scott, The Antiquary was a prized luxury blend in its heyday. Befitting its deluxe status, it has at its heart a very high malt-to-grain ratio, including some of the finest malts from Speyside and Highland distilleries and more than a splash of Tomatin. Islay seems to feature more strongly than previously.

◄ THE ANTIQUARY 12-YEAR-OLD

BLEND 40% ABV

Subtle fruitiness concealing a hint of apples. Outstanding smoothness, depth of flavor, and a long aftertaste. Other tasters have reported a striking peat influence, new to the blend.

THE ANTIQUARY 21-YEAR-OLD

BLEND 43% ABV

The subtle maltiness with muted peaty notes allows the heather, dandelion, and black currant notes to flourish. A dash of Islay malt creates a truly exceptional dram: well-balanced, rich, and smooth. A standout blend that deserves to be more widely enjoyed.

ARDBEG

Scotland
Port Ellen, Islay
www.ardbeg.com

If Islay is the spiritual home of Scotland's pungent, peat-smoked whiskies, then Ardbeg is undoubtedly one of the island's leading disciples. The distillery was first licensed in 1815 in the parish of Kildalton, on Islay's southern coast just beyond Lagavulin and Laphroaig.

Reliance on the blending market left Ardbeg in a vulnerable position, however, and when "the whisky loch" became full to the brim in the early 1980s, the distillery was mothballed.

ARDBEG 10-YEAR-OLD ▶
SINGLE MALT: ISLAY 46% ABV
This non–chill filtered malt has notes of creosote, tar, and smoked fish on the nose. Any sweetness on the tongue quickly dries to a smoky finish.

ARDBEG AIRIGH NAM BEIST
SINGLE MALT: ISLAY 46% ABV
A rich, spicy malt sweetened with vanilla notes from 16 years in bourbon casks. The name, pronounced *arry nam bayst*, means "shelter of the beast."

ARDBEG

In 1997, Ardbeg was rescued by Glenmorangie, who paid a reported $11.5m and then spent a further $2.3m on upgrading the distillery. At first, the years of non-production caused problems but, as the gaps in the inventory receded, the distillery was finally able to release a standard 10-year-old bottling. Since then, there has been a raft of new bottlings, which have added to Ardbeg's growing cult status among fans of Islay's smoky malt whiskies.

◀ ARDBEG BLASDA

SINGLE MALT: ISLAY 40% ABV
The Gaelic name translates as "sweet and delicious," a reference to a much gentler style than usual, made from malt peated at only 8ppm, one-third Ardbeg's usual levels.

ARDBEG UIGEADAIL

SINGLE MALT: ISLAY 54.2% ABV
Named after Loch Uigeadail—Ardbeg's water source—this has a deep gold color and a molasseslike sweetness on the nose, with savory, smoky notes following through on the tongue.

THE ARDMORE

Scotland
Kennethmont, Aberdeenshire
www.ardmorewhisky.com

Ardmore owes its existence
to Teacher's Highland Cream
(*see p341*). The Teacher's blend
was well-established in Scotland,
particularly in Glasgow, where it
was sold through Teacher's Dram
Shops, and sales were growing
abroad. To keep up with demand,
Adam Teacher decided to build
a new distillery in 1898 and found
the ideal spot near Kennethmont,
beside the main Aberdeen-to-
Inverness railroad. Famed for
producing the smokiest malt
on Speyside, Ardmore released
a 12-year-old in 1999 to celebrate
its centenary. In 2005 the
distillery became part of
Fortune Brands.

ARDMORE
TRADITIONAL CASK ▶

SINGLE MALT: SPEYSIDE
46% ABV

A smooth, relatively full-bodied malt,
where the sweet American oak flavors
from the cask are balanced by the dry,
earthy character from the peat.

A

ARMORIK

France

Distillerie Warenghem,
Route de Guingamp,
22300 Lannion, Bretagne
www.distillerie-warenghem.com

The Warenghem Distillery was founded in 1900 to produce apple cider and fruit spirits. It was not until 99 years later that the owners decided to start making other types of spirits, including malted beers and whisky. There are now two types of whisky made here: Armorik, a single malt, and WB (Whisky Breton), a blend. The type of casks used for maturation is not specified.

◀ ARMORIK WHISKY BRETON CLASSIC

SINGLE MALT 46% ABV

Citrus fruits, spicy malt, hazelnuts, and vanilla on the nose, while the full, oily palate yields malt, honey, vanilla, and dried fruits, before a spicy and slightly salty finish.

THE ARRAN MALT

Scotland

Lochranza, Isle of Arran
www.arranwhisky.com

When the distillery opened in 1993, it marked the return of distilling on the Isle of Arran after a hiatus of some 156 years. Arran uses water from Loch na Davie on the island's north coast, and the island itself is positioned in the Gulf Stream, where the warm waters and climate system are said to beneficially speed up the maturation period. Arran creates a range of blends named for Robert Burns, who was born nearby on the mainland (*see p297*).

ARRAN 10-YEAR-OLD ▶

SINGLE MALT: ISLANDS 46% ABV
Bottled without chill filtering, this has fresh bread and vanilla aromas, with citrus notes that carry through onto the tongue.

ARRAN 12-YEAR-OLD

SINGLE MALT: ISLANDS 46% ABV
This expression has a chocolate sweetness and a rich, creamy texture thanks to the influence of sherry wood.

AUCHENTOSHAN

Scotland
Dalmuir, Clydebank, Glasgow
www.auchentoshan.com

While Glenkinchie sits just south of Edinburgh, Scotland's other main Lowlands distillery lies west of Glasgow by the Erskine Bridge and the Clyde River.

Auchentoshan, licensed in 1823, produced a modest 50,000 gallons (225,000 liters) a year with a single pair of stills until it acquired a third still. Ever since, Auchentoshan, with its triple-distilled malt, has been almost unique in Scotland. This being the

◀ AUCHENTOSHAN AMERICAN OAK

SINGLE MALT: LOWLANDS 40% ABV
An initial note of rosewater, developing musky peaches, and icing sugar. Spicy, fresh fruit on the palate, chili notes, and more vanilla.

AUCHENTOSHAN 12-YEAR-OLD

SINGLE MALT: LOWLANDS 40% ABV
This expression replaced the old 10-year-old and has a dense, spicy character thanks to the use of sherry casks.

standard style of Irish whiskey, it soon caught on among the burgeoning Irish community in Glasgow.

The Clydebank area was a key target for the Luftwaffe in World War II and, after some heavy bombing in 1941, Auchentoshan has since drawn its cooling water from a pond created in a giant bomb crater.

Auchentoshan joined forces with the Islay distillery Bowmore in 1984, becoming Morrison Bowmore, now part Suntory. In the past decade, the range of single malts has been greatly expanded.

AUCHENTOSHAN THREE WOOD ▶

SINGLE MALT: LOWLANDS 43% ABV
This is matured in three different types of cask, and sherry clearly has a big influence on the color and sweet, candied-fruit flavors.

AUCHENTOSHAN 18-YEAR-OLD

SINGLE MALT: LOWLANDS 43% ABV
This is a classic nutty, spicy malt with plenty of age and complexity on the palate and some fruity sherry notes on the nose.

AULTMORE

Scotland

Keith, Banffshire
Owner: John Dewar & Sons (Bacardi)

Alexander Edward was a seasoned distiller at Benrinnes before establishing the Craigellachie Distillery with Peter Mackie, the whisky baron and founder of the White Horse blend. In 1895, at the peak of the late-Victorian whisky boom, Edward built Aultmore on the flat farmland between Keith and the sea. After acquisition by John Dewar & Sons and DCL, the distillery was one of five sold to Bacardi in 1998. Over 2014 and 2015 the range was revamped and expanded.

◀ AULTMORE 12-YEAR-OLD

SINGLE MALT: SPEYSIDE 46% ABV
A nose of peaches and lemonade, freshly mown grass, linseed, and milky coffee. Very fruity on the palate, mildly herbal, with toffee and light spices.

AULTMORE 18-YEAR-OLD

SINGLE MALT: SPEYSIDE 46% ABV
Vanilla, new-mown hay, and contrasting lemon notes on the nose, while the nicely textured palate offers more lemon, along with orange and malt.

BAGPIPER

India
Owner: United Spirits
www.unitedspirits.in

"The World's No.1 Non-Scotch Whisky" sells nearly 14 million cases a year. An IMFL (Indian Made Foreign Liquor), probably made from molasses alcohol and concentrates, it was launched by the United Spirits subsidiary Herbertson's in 1987 and, in its first year, sold 100,000 cases. The brand has always been closely associated with Bollywood, India's huge film-production industry, and has successfully won accreditation from many movie stars. The company also broadcasts a weekly Bagpiper show on TV, and is a sponsor of talent-spotting programs.

BAGPIPER GOLD ▶

BLEND 42.8% ABV

Gold is the premium expression of Bagpiper, but it still has a somewhat artificial taste and is best drunk with a mixer like cola.

BAKER'S

US

Jim Beam Distillery,
149 Happy Hollow Road,
Clermont, Kentucky
www.jimbeam.com

Baker's is one of three whiskeys that were introduced in 1992 as Beam's Small Batch Bourbon Collection. It is named after Baker Beam, the former Clermont Master Distiller and grand-nephew of the legendary Jim Beam himself. He is also a cousin of the late Booker Noe, the high-profile distiller who instigated small-batch bourbon distilling. Baker Beam's namesake whiskey is distilled using the standard Jim Beam formula, but is aged for longer and offered at a higher bottling strength.

◀ **BAKER'S 7-YEAR-OLD**

BOURBON 53.5% ABV

Baker's is a fruity, toasty expression of the Jim Beam formula: medium-bodied, mellow, and richly flavored, with notes of vanilla and caramel.

BAKERY HILL

Australia

28 Ventnor Street,
North Balwyn, Victoria
www.bakeryhilldistillery.com.au

David Baker, chemist and founder of Bakery Hill Distillery, was determined to prove that top-quality malt whisky could be made in Australia. He has succeeded: his single cask, non–chill filtered malts are already winning awards. The barley strains Australian Franklin and Australian Schooner are sourced locally and sometimes malted over locally cut peat. Bakery Hill whiskies are now available well beyond their homeland, near Melbourne, Victoria.

BAKERY HILL CASK STRENGTH PEATED MALT ▶

SINGLE MALT 59.88% ABV
Intense peatiness on the nose, with dark cherry. The taste is sweet (toffee, honeycomb), with some salt and smoke. It has a good texture.

BAKERY HILL PEATED MALT

SINGLE MALT 46% ABV
A sweet and oaky balance of peat and malt on the nose. These aromas carry through in the taste.

BALBLAIR

Scotland

Edderton, Tain, Ross-shire
www.balblair.com

Founded in 1790 by John Ross, Balblair is one of only a handful of 18th-century distilleries that has survived to this day. It remained in family hands for over 100 years. Since 1996, the distillery has been owned by Inver House Distillers, who began with a core range called Elements. This was succeeded by a range of vintage malts in a similar style to The Glenrothes bottlings, right down to the bulbous bottle shape.

◀ BALBLAIR 90

SINGLE MALT: HIGHLANDS 46% ABV
The nose is rich, sherried, and spicy, with leather and fruit. Smooth and full on the palate, with honey and spicy sherry. Drying oak in the persistently spicy finish.

BALBLAIR 99

SINGLE MALT: HIGHLANDS 46% ABV
Floral on the nose, with ripe apples, light sherry, and furniture polish. The palate is sweet and rounded, with honey and warm leather.

BALCONES

US

Balcones Distilling,
212 S. 17th Street, Waco, Texas
www.balconesdistilling.com

Balcones was established in 2008 by Chip Tate, but he has since parted company with the venture and plans to create a new distillery in the near future. From the outset, Balcones was synonymous with the more experimental side of microdistilling, producing products such as the "Texas Scrub Oak Smoked" corn whiskey Brimstone, and Baby Blue, made from roasted heirloom blue corn. The innovative company's bestseller is its Texas Single Malt Whisky.

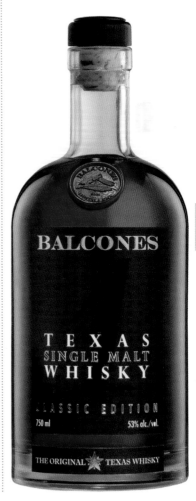

BALCONES TEXAS SINGLE MALT ▶

SINGLE MALT 53% ABV

Toffee, honey, and creamy vanilla on the nose. Malt, honey, apples, and cinnamon on the palate, with closing spicy oak.

BALLANTINE'S

Scotland
www.ballantines.com

Ballantine's was a pioneer in developing aged blends. Its range is arguably the most extensive in the world today, and includes Ballantine's Finest (the standard bottling), as well as Ballantine's 12-year-old, 17-year-old, 21-year-old, and 30-year-old. The range is the world's second biggest Scotch whisky by volume and the top-selling super-premium brand in Asia.

The blend is noted for its complexity, with over 40 different malts and grains being used. The two Speyside single malts

◄ BALLANTINE'S FINEST
BLEND 40% ABV

A sweet, soft-textured blend, with the Speyside malts giving chocolate, vanilla, and apple notes.

BALLANTINE'S 12-YEAR-OLD
BLEND 40% ABV

Golden-hued, with a honey sweetness on the nose, and vanilla from the oak. Creamy texture and balanced palate, with floral, honey, and oaky vanilla notes. Some tasters detect a hint of salt.

Glenburgie and Miltonduff form the base for the blend, but malts from all parts of Scotland are also employed. For maturation, Ballantine's principally favors the use of ex-bourbon barrels, for the vanilla influences and sweet creamy notes they characteristically bring to the blend.

The Glenburgie Distillery has been completely remodeled and modernized and is today Ballantine's spiritual home.

BALLANTINE'S 21-YEAR-OLD ▶
BLEND 43% ABV

The sought-after older expressions of Ballantine's are deep in color, with traces of heather, smoke, licorice, and spice on the nose. The 21-year-old has a complex, balanced palate, with sherry, honey, and floral notes.

BALLANTINE'S 17-YEAR-OLD
BLEND 43% ABV

A deep, balanced, and elegant whisky with a hint of wood and vanilla. The body is full and creamy, with a vibrant, honeyed sweetness and hints of oak and peat smoke on the palate.

BALMENACH

Scotland

*Cromdale, Grantown-on-Spey,
Morayshire*
www.inverhouse.com

In 1824 James McGregor, like
many illicit distillers, decided
to come in from the cold and take
out a license for his farm distillery
near Grantown-on-Spey. It was
owned by the family for 100
years until they sold to DCL.
Aside from during World War II,
the distillery was in constant
production until 1993, when its
whisky was available as part of
the Flora & Fauna range. In 1997,
Balmenach was sold to Inver
House, who fired up the stills
the following year. A full distillery
bottling has had to wait, owing
to a dearth of inherited stocks.

◀ BALMENACH GORDON & MACPHAIL 1990

SINGLE MALT: SPEYSIDE 43% ABV
Citrus, grass, and malt on the nose,
slight smoke on the palate. Opens
up with water.

THE BALVENIE

Scotland

Dufftown, Keith, Banffshire
www.thebalvenie.com

Within six years of setting up
Glenfiddich in 1886, William
Grant was converting Balvenie
New House (a derelict Georgian
pile) next door into another
distillery using second-hand stills.
This expansion was partly a result
of a request from an Aberdeen
blender who desperately needed
400 gallons (1,800 liters) of
Glenlivet-style whisky a week. ☞

THE BALVENIE DOUBLEWOOD 12-YEAR-OLD ▶

SINGLE MALT: SPEYSIDE 40% ABV
After a decade in American oak,
Doublewood spends two years in
ex-sherry casks to give it a smooth,
confected, slightly nutty character.

THE BALVENIE PORTWOOD 21-YEAR-OLD

SINGLE MALT: SPEYSIDE 40% ABV
The nose is soft and creamy, with ripe
fruits, and a smoky, musky red wine
note. Full-bodied and rich on the
palate. Subtly spiced, drying to nutty
oak, with fruity wine notes on the finish.

SINGLE MALT SCOTCH WHISKY

Distilled at

THE BALVENIE®

Distillery, Banffshire

AGED 30 YEARS

MALT MASTER DAVID STEWART HAS MARRIED TOGETHER BALVENIE MATURED
OVER THREE DECADES IN TRADITIONAL AND EUROPEAN OAK CASKS TO CREATE
A SINGLE MALT WITH UNUSUAL DEPTH AND COMPLEXITY

David Stewart

DAVID STEWART, THE BALVENIE MALT MASTER

THE BALVENIE DISTILLERY COMPANY
BALVENIE MALTINGS, DUFFTOWN, BANFFSHIRE, SCOTLAND AB55 4BB

THE BALVENIE

Although physically dwarfed by Glenfiddich, Balvenie is no boutique distillery: it can produce 1.5 million gallons (6.8 million liters) a year and has built up an impressive range of single malts. As an artisan distillery, it claims to grow some of its own barley, in contrast to Glenfiddich. It has also retained its floor maltings to satisfy part of its requirements, and employs a coppersmith and a team of coopers. Indeed, Balvenie's attention to maturation and different wood finishes rivals even that of Glenmorangie.

◀ THE BALVENIE 30-YEAR-OLD

SINGLE MALT: SPEYSIDE 47.3% ABV
The nose features caramel, nutmeg, figs, Jaffa oranges, and spicy oak, while the rich palate offers honey, spice, ripe plums, and supple oak.

THE BALVENIE CARIBBEAN CASK 14-YEAR-OLD

SINGLE MALT: SPEYSIDE 43% ABV
Toffee, orchard fruits, and white rum on the nose, while the rounded palate yields sugary malt, more fruit, vanilla, and soft oak. The finish is medium in length, with gently spiced oak.

BARTON

300 Barton Road, Bardstown, Kentucky
Owner: Sazerac

Bardstown is in the true heartland of bourbon, and once boasted more than 20 distilleries. Barton's whiskeys are typically youthful, dry, and aromatic.

In 2009, the Sazerac Company Inc, which also owns Buffalo Trace, acquired the Tom Moore Distillery from Constellation Brands, as well as all the Barton whiskeys produced there, including Very Old Barton, Kentucky Gentleman *(see p207),* Ridgemont *(p295),* Kentucky Tavern, Ten High, and Tom Moore.

VERY OLD BARTON ▶
BOURBON 43% ABV
This brand used to boast an age statement of six years, but this has now been dropped. The nose is rich, syrupy, and spicy, with a prickle of salt. Big-bodied in the mouth, it is fruity and spicy, with spices and ginger in the drying finish.

WHISKEYS

B

GREAT

37

BASIL HAYDEN'S

US

Jim Beam Distillery,
149 Happy Hollow Road,
Clermont, Kentucky
www.basilhaydens.com

Basil Hayden's was one of the three whiskeys that made up Beam's pioneering Small Batch Bourbon Collection, introduced in 1992. Basil Hayden was an early Kentucky settler from Maryland who began making whiskey in the late 18th century near Bardstown, and it is claimed that the recipe for this particular expression dates from that period.

◀ BASIL HAYDEN'S 8-YEAR-OLD

BOURBON 40% ABV

The nose is light, aromatic, and spicy, with flavors of soft rye, wood polish, spices, pepper, vanilla, and a hint of honey on the comparatively dry palate. The finish is long, with notes of peppery rye.

THE BELGIAN OWL

Belgium

The Owl Distillery,
Rue Sainte Anne 94,
B4460 Grâce-Hollogne
www.belgianwhisky.com

Master Distiller Etienne Bouillon founded this distillery in the French-speaking part of Belgium in 2004. He uses home-grown barley and first-fill bourbon casks to produce a 3-year-old single malt whisky. The first batch was bottled in the fall of 2007. The Belgian Owl Distillery was formerly known under the names Lambicool and PUR-E.

BELGIAN SINGLE MALT ▶

SINGLE MALT 46% ABV

This non–chill filtered malt offers vanilla, coconut, banana, and ice cream, topped with fig, followed by a crescendo of other flavors such as lemon, apples, and ginger. A long finish, with ripe fruits and vanilla.

BELL'S

Scotland
www.bells.co.uk

"Several fine whiskies blended together please the palates of a greater number of people than one whisky unmixed," wrote the first Arthur Bell. In keeping with this spirit, the current owners of Bell's, Diageo, lay great emphasis on the skill of the blenders. Bell's acquired Blair Athol (the source of the single malt at the heart of the blend) and Dufftown distilleries in 1933, adding Inchgower in 1936. The blend always evolves: the company insists that, in blind taste tests, drinkers prefer the new version.

◀ BELL'S ORIGINAL
BLEND 40% ABV
As well as Blair Athol, Dufftown and Inchgower are important components here, along with Glenkinchie and Caol Ila. Medium-bodied blend, with a nutty aroma and a lightly spiced flavor.

BELL'S SPECIAL RESERVE
BLEND 40% ABV
Special Reserve has smoky hints from the Islay malts, tempered with warm pepper and a rich honey complexity.

BEN NEVIS

Scotland

Lochy Bridge, Fort William
www.bennevisdistillery.com

Scotland's most northerly west coast distillery was founded in 1825 by "Long John" MacDonald, who was the inspiration for the once-popular blend of that name (*see p233*). Sitting by Loch Linnhe, Fort William, the 19th century distillery even had its own small fleet of steamers to ferry the whisky down the loch.

Periodic closures during the 1970s and 80s have caused gaps in its inventory, but despite this, a number of older single malts have been released alongside the various Dew of Ben Nevis blends. Since the mid-1990s, the core single malt has been the 10-year-old, augmented in 2011 by the MacDonald's Traditional.

BEN NEVIS 10-YEAR-OLD ▶

SINGLE MALT: HIGHLANDS 46% ABV

A big, mouth-filling West Highlands malt with a sweet smack of oak and an oily texture that finishes dry.

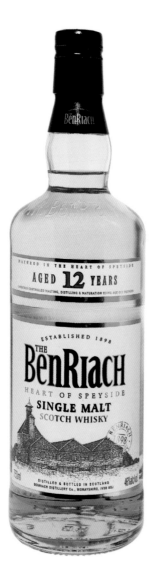

BENRIACH

Scotland

Longmorn, Elgin, Morayshire
www.benriachdistillery.co.uk

Of all the Speyside distilleries built on the crest of the great speculative wave of whisky-making at the end of the 19th century, few crashed so badly as BenRiach. It opened in 1897 but only operated until 1903, when it was closed for the first half of the 20th century. Then, in 1965, after a major refurbishment, its pair of stills was fired up again. Its subsequent owners, Seagram, having no distillery on Islay, decided to

◀ BENRIACH 12-YEAR-OLD

SINGLE MALT: SPEYSIDE 40% ABV
More classically Speyside in character than the 10-year-old, with a heathery nose, creamy vanilla ice cream flavor, and a hint of honey.

BENRIACH CURIOSITAS 10-YEAR-OLD

SINGLE MALT: SPEYSIDE 40% ABV
A bitter-sweet whisky with a dense peaty flavor. Beneath the smoke, there are flavors of cookies, cereal, and some citrus notes.

produce a powerful peat-smoked malt at BenRiach in 1983. There were still some stocks of this peated BenRiach left when a South African consortium led by Billy Walker took over in 2004 from Chivas Brothers. This led to the Curiositas and Authenticus bottlings—the only commercially available Speyside single malts distilled from peated malted barley.

With 5,000 different casks dating back to 1970 and different levels of peating to play with, Billy Walker has been able to dramatically expand the range of BenRiach malts available.

BENRIACH 16-YEAR-OLD ▶

SINGLE MALT: SPEYSIDE 40% ABV
A nutty, spicy Speysider, with a honeyed texture in the mouth and perhaps the faintest wisp of smoke.

BENRIACH 20-YEAR-OLD

SINGLE MALT: SPEYSIDE 40% ABV
The long years in oak have given this expression a dry, woody flavor, with sharp citrus notes and a clean finish.

BENRINNES

Scotland

Aberlour, Banffshire
www.malts.com

The original Benrinnes
Distillery was founded in 1826
at Whitehouse Farm on lower
Speyside by Peter McKenzie,
but was swept away in a flood
three years later. In 1834 a new
distillery called the Lyne of
Ruthrie was built a few miles
away and, despite bankruptcies
and a bad fire in 1896, it has
survived as Benrinnes. What you
see today is a modern post-war
distillery, which was completely
rebuilt in the mid-1950s. It has six
stills that operate a partial form of
triple distillation, with one wash
still paired with two spirit stills.

◀ BENRINNES FLORA & FAUNA 15-YEAR-OLD

SINGLE MALT: SPEYSIDE 43% ABV
The only official distillery bottling
is fairly sumptuous, with some
smoke and spicy flavors and a
creamy mouthfeel.

BENROMACH

Scotland
Forres, Morayshire
www.benromach.com

With just a single pair of stills and
a maximum production of 110,000
gallons (500,000 liters) of pure
alcohol a year, Benromach was
always something of a pint-size
distillery. It was founded in 1898
and changed hands no fewer than
six times in its first 100 years. At
one point, it found itself part of
National Distillers of America,
sharing a stable with bourbon
brands such as Old Crow and
Old Grand-Dad. ☞

BENROMACH 10-YEAR-OLD ▶
SINGLE MALT: SPEYSIDE 43% ABV
Smoky on the nose, with wet grass,
butter, ginger, and brittle toffee.
Mouth-coating, spicy, and nutty on
the palate, with raisins, and soft
wood smoke.

BENROMACH 15-YEAR-OLD
SINGLE MALT: SPEYSIDE 43% ABV
Nutty and spicy on the nose, with
dried fruits, sherry, and orange. More
orange on the palate, with ginger and
milk chocolate, leading into smoky,
spicy oak.

BENROMACH

Then, like so many dispossessed distilleries, Benromach became part of the giant DCL, who mothballed the distillery in 1983. The stills were ripped out and it seemed Benromach would never produce whisky again.

Benromach's savior was the famous firm of independent bottlers Gordon & MacPhail of Elgin, who bought the distillery in 1993. A new pair of stills was installed, and the first spirit flowed from it in 1999, when Prince Charles officially opened the new Benromach.

In line with many Speyside single malts of old, there is an element of peatiness about the spirit.

◀ BENROMACH 35-YEARS-OLD

SINGLE MALT: SPEYSIDE 43% ABV
The nose is warm and floral, with sherry and faint smoke in time. Smooth, spicy, and lightly smoky on the palate, drying to spicy tannins.

BENROMACH 100 PROOF

SINGLE MALT: SPEYSIDE 57% ABV
Sherry, vanilla, chili, and dried fruits on the nose. Long and smoky finish.

BERNHEIM

US

Heaven Hill Distillery,
1701 West Breckinridge Street,
Louisville, Kentucky
www.bernheimwheatwhiskey.com

The Bernheim brand takes its name from Heaven Hill's Bernheim Distillery in Louisville, Kentucky, where Heaven Hill whiskeys have been produced since the plant was acquired in 1999. Launched in 2005, Bernheim is the only straight wheat whiskey on the US market.

Heaven Hill father and son Master Distillers Parker and Craig Beam developed the wheat formula with a minimum of 51 percent winter wheat, and the recipe also includes corn and malted barley.

BERNHEIM ORIGINAL ▶
WHEAT WHISKEY 45% ABV
Bernheim exhibits light fruit notes on the spicy nose, with freshly sawn wood, toffee, vanilla, sweetish grain, and a hint of mint on the palate. A long, elegant, honeyed, and spicy finish.

BLACK & WHITE

Scotland
Owner: Diageo

A fondly regarded brand from the Buchanan's stable, Black & White originally went by the name Buchanan's Special. The story goes that, in the 1890s, James Buchanan supplied his whisky to the House of Commons in a very dark bottle with a white label. Apparently incapable of memorizing the name, British parliamentarians simply called for "Black and White." Buchanan adopted the name and subsequently adorned the label with two dogs—a black Scottish terrier and a white West Highland terrier. Today it is marketed by Diageo in France, Brazil, and Venezuela, where it continues to enjoy a popularity long since lost in its homeland.

◀ **BLACK & WHITE**
BLEND 40% ABV
A high-class, traditional-style blend. Layered hints of peat, smoke, and oak.

48

BLACK BOTTLE

Scotland

Owner: Burn Stewart Distillers
www.blackbottle.com

Black Bottle was created in 1879
by C., D., & G. Grahams, a firm of
Aberdeen tea blenders. Grahams
ran the company for almost 90
years before it was eventually sold
in 1964. The Black Bottle brand
changed hands several times
before being bought in 2003
by Burn Stewart Distillers as
part of their purchase of the
Bunnahabhain distillery. In 2013,
Burn Stewart relaunched the
brand, giving less prominence to
malts from Islay by including more
Speyside-style characteristics,
taking it closer to its northeast
roots.

BLACK BOTTLE ▶

BLEND 40% ABV
Fresh oak, light smoke, honey, and
a hint of sherry on the nose. Caramel,
berry fruits, honey, and more light
smoke on the palate, with plain
chocolate and drying oak.

BLACK VELVET

Canada
*2925 9th Avenue North,
Lethbridge, Alberta
www.blackvelvetwhisky.com*

Black Velvet is the third best-selling Canadian whisky in the US. It was created by Gilbey Canada in the 1950s as Black Label, and made at the Old Palliser Distillery in Toronto. It was so successful that, in 1973, the Black Velvet Distillery was established at Lethbridge, in the shadow of the Rockies, only a couple of hours drive from the US border. In 1999, both Black Velvet and Palliser were sold to Barton Brands, then later became part of Constellation Brands.

◄ BLACK VELVET RESERVE
BLEND 40% ABV

A light and mellow nose with vanilla notes. The palate is mild and sweet, with butterscotch, a faint citrus note, and light spiciness. Velvet-smooth texture, but the flavor lacks depth.

BLADNOCH

Scotland

Bladnoch, Wigtown, Wigtonshire
www.bladnoch.com

Scotland's most southerly
distillery has been bought and
sold several times, spending
long periods lying idle in between.
Finally, Guinness UDV (now
Diageo) sold it in 1994. The deal
brokered was that Bladnoch would
never produce whisky again, but
in 2000 they relented and the
distillery was allowed to produce
250,000 bottles a year. In 2009,
Bladnoch was once again
mothballed until the distillery
was acquired in 2015 by
Australian entrepreneur David
Prior. Production was officially
restarted in June 2017.

BLADNOCH 15-YEAR-OLD ▶

SINGLE MALT: LOWLANDS 55% ABV
A light, crisp, apéritif-style whisky
with a trace of green apples.

BLADNOCH 18-YEAR-OLD

SINGLE MALT: LOWLANDS 55% ABV
This smooth lowland malt is bottled
at full cask strength without chill
filtration, but is in short supply.

BLAIR ATHOL

Scotland
Pitlochry, Perthshire
www.malts.com

In 1798 John Stewart and Robert Robertson took out a license for their Aldour Distillery on the edge of Pitlochry. In an area crawling with illicit stills, life was tough for legitimate, tax-paying distilleries, and Aldour soon closed. It was resurrected in 1826 by Alexander Connacher, who renamed it Blair Athol. Within 30 years, some of the malt was being sold to the Perth blender Arthur Bell & Sons, who finally bought the distillery in 1933 *(see p41)*. Except for the 12-year-old and the occasional rare malt, nearly every drop goes into blends, particularly Bell's.

◀ BLAIR ATHOL FLORA & FAUNA 12-YEAR-OLD
SINGLE MALT: HIGHLANDS 43% ABV
Smooth, well-rounded flavors, with spice and candied fruit, and a trace of smoke on the finish.

BLANTON'S

US
*Buffalo Trace,
1001 Wilkinson Boulevard,
Frankfort, Kentucky*
www.buffalotrace.com

Colonel Albert Bacon Blanton
worked for no fewer than 55 years
at what is now the Buffalo Trace
Distillery, starting as office boy in
1897 and graduating to distillery
manager in 1912. When he retired
in 1955, the distillery was
renamed Blanton's in his honor.
This single barrel expression was
created in 1984 by Master Distiller
Elmer T. Lee, who worked with
Blanton during the 1950s.

BLANTON'S SINGLE BARREL ▶

BOURBON 46.5% ABV

The nose of Blanton's is soft, with
toffee, leather, and a hint of mint.
Full-bodied and rounded on the palate,
this is a notably sweet bourbon,
embracing vanilla, caramel, honey, and
spices. The finish is long and creamy,
with a hint of late spice.

BLAUE MAUS

Germany

Fleischmann, Bamberger Straße 2, 91330 Eggolsheim-Neuses
www.fleischmann-whisky.de

The Fleischmann brandy distillery was founded in 1980 on the premises of the original family company—a grocery and tobacco shop. In 1996, after nearly 14 years of experimentation with whisky distillation, the company launched their first whisky expression. There are now eight different single cask malt whiskies available, including Blaue Maus, Grüner Hund, and Old Fahr, along with a single cask grain whisky—Austrasier.

◀ BLAUE MAUS OLD FAHR

SINGLE MALT 40% ABV
The nose offers plain chocolate, ginger, and a slight oiliness. The oiliness continues onto the soft palate, which features contrasting vanilla and drying oak notes, with plain chocolate returning in the finish.

BLENDERS PRIDE

India
Owner: Pernod Ricard
www.pernod-ricard.com

Since it fell under the ownership of Pernod Ricard, this brand has been neck and neck with Royal Challenge (*see p305*) as the bestseller in its sector. It is a premium IMFL (Indian Made Foreign Liquor, made from Scotch malts and Indian grains), whose name comes from a story about the master blenders who exposed a cask of whisky to the warmth of the sun at regular intervals. The delicate sweetness and aromatic flavor of the blend are testimony to the success of their experiment.

BLENDERS PRIDE ▶
BLEND 42.8% ABV
A smooth and rich mouthfeel, with a sweet taste that gives way to a disappointingly dull finish.

BOOKER'S

US

Jim Beam Distillery,
149 Happy Hollow Road,
Clermont, Kentucky
www.bookersbourbon.com

A brand created by the global Jim Beam company, Booker's is named after Jim Beam's grandson, Booker Noe. Booker was a sixth-generation Master Distiller and the man credited with the introduction of "small batch" bourbon in 1992. On their website, Booker's declare that of the few batches they release every year, "each varies in age and proof because reaching Booker's standards is a mix of art, science and Mother Nature. It tells us when it's ready, and then we'll let you know."

◀ BOOKER'S 2015 BATCH OF NOE'S SECRET

BOURBON 64.05% ABV
Richly aromatic nose of vanilla, corn, and cinnamon. Caramel and more vanilla on the palate, with big spice notes, char, oak, and raspberries.

BOWMORE

Scotland
Bowmore, Isle of Islay
www.bowmore.co.uk

The oldest surviving distillery on
Islay was founded in 1779. The
distillery remained small for years,
until the Glasgow firm of W. & J.
Mutter bought it in 1837,
increasing its annual production
to 200,000 gallons (900,000 liters)
and storing the casks in their
warehouse beneath Glasgow's
Central Station. In 1963 it was
bought by Glasgow broker Stanley
P. Morrison and today is the
flagship distillery of Morrison
Bowmore, itself part of the
Japanese drinks giant Suntory. ☞

BOWMORE 12-YEAR-OLD ▶
SINGLE MALT: ISLAY 40% ABV
Gently aromatic, with a mix of citrus
fruits and smoke on the nose, which
carries through to the tongue, together
with some dark chocolate.

BOWMORE LEGEND
SINGLE MALT: ISLAY 40% ABV
Dry and bracing, with a faint
citrus flavor that develops into
a smoky finish.

BOWMORE

Bowmore stands on the shores of Loch Indaal. With the salty sea breeze blowing right into the warehouses, some of it is bound to seep into the casks. The distillery has two pairs of stills, six Oregon-pine washbacks, and its own floor maltings, which can supply up to 40 percent of Bowmore's needs. Whether using its own malt, which is peated to around 25 ppm, improves the flavor of Bowmore would be hard to prove, but to see the whole process, from the freshly steeped barley to the peat-fired kiln and its dense blue smoke, certainly makes a visit to the Bowmore Distillery that much more special.

◀ BOWMORE 15-YEAR-OLD
SINGLE MALT: ISLAY 43% ABV
The deep mahogany color comes from two years in Oloroso casks, which also give a raisinlike sweetness to Bowmore's signature note of smoke.

BOWMORE 17-YEAR-OLD
SINGLE MALT: ISLAY 43% ABV
Rich caramel on the nose with a background of peat. Creamy texture, with malt, peat, and fruit interplay on the palate, and a long, warming finish.

BOX

Sweden
Sörviken 140, 872 96 Bjärtrå
www.boxwhisky.se

The Box Distillery came on stream
in 2010, situated at the old Box
Power Station, constructed in
1912 in the heart of the Ädalen
region of Sweden. The distillery
has two conventional, Scottish-
built pot stills and produces two
styles of spirit—one unpeated,
the other peated with imported
Islay peat.

Box has issued a number of
limited-edition bottlings to date,
and they have been met with
great enthusiasm from Swedish
whisky fans. The Pioneer, released
in 2014, sold out its 5,000-bottle
run in only seven hours.

BOX MESSENGER ▶
SINGLE MALT 48.4% ABV
Matured in a mix of bourbon and
Oloroso sherry casks, with a
proportion of peated spirit. Pears,
bananas, and vanilla on the nose, with
a hint of peat. Pepper and salt on the
herbal palate, finishing with banana.

Whiskey Tour:
ISLAY

The Hebridean island of Islay is the destination for "peat freaks," particularly during the annual malt and music festival, Fèis Ìle, in May. You can either fly to Islay from Glasgow then rent a car to get around, or use the Caledonian MacBrayne ferry from Kennacraig to bring your own vehicle. A four-day itinerary should take in all eight distilleries.

DAY 1: CAOL ILA, BUNNAHABHAIN

❶ If arriving in Port Askaig by ferry, the logical place to stay is the charming, family-run Port Askaig Hotel on the coast. From there you can walk to **Caol Ila**, a large Diageo distillery that is the most highly productive on the island.

❷ It's a car trip or hike along the coastal path from Port Askaig to **Bunnahabhain**, which makes the most lightly peated of the Islay whiskies. It is possible to rent one of the distillery cottages to stay in.

WASHBACKS AT CAOL ILA

DAY 2: KILCHOMAN, BRUICHLADDICH

❸ Tiny **Kilchoman** is Islay's newest and smallest distillery. It's also a farm with a friendly café. Like other Islay distilleries, it sells special bottlings that may not be available elsewhere. This is a great spot for lunch and the dishes use locally sourced ingredients.

❹ Drive back over the hill to **Bruichladdich**, which produces a huge array of whiskies. It is near Port Charlotte, where you can learn about illicit whisky production in the Museum of Islay Life, then enjoy dinner at the Port Charlotte Hotel.

BRUICHLADDICH

SCOTLAND

B8018

KILCHOMAN **❸**

BRUICHLADDICH **❹**

PORT CHARLOTTE

miles
0   2

0   2
kilometers

TOUR STATISTICS

DAYS: 4
LENGTH: 60 miles (96km)
TRAVEL: Car, walking
DISTILLERIES: 8

DAY 3: LAPHROAIG, LAGAVULIN, ARDBEG

❺ The Kildalton distilleries, as these three are known, are renowned for their strong peaty character. **Laphroaig** is reputedly Prince Charles's favorite dram. The distillery tour includes the splendidly maintained maltings.

❻ From Laphroaig, take a five-minute stroll to **Lagavulin** to compare these two single malts with their assertive peaty flavors.

❼ Lastly, there's **Ardbeg**, where lunch at the Old Kiln Café is not to be missed. If you like history, there's a fine 8th-century cross on the road to Kildalton.

MODEL IN LAGAVULIN'S DRAM ROOM

DAY 4: BOWMORE

❽ Spend your last morning at **Bowmore** Distillery, where you can visit the floor maltings and visitor center. Repair to the Harbour Inn for a final lunch before catching the afternoon ferry from Port Askaig back to the mainland.

BOWMORE WAREHOUSE

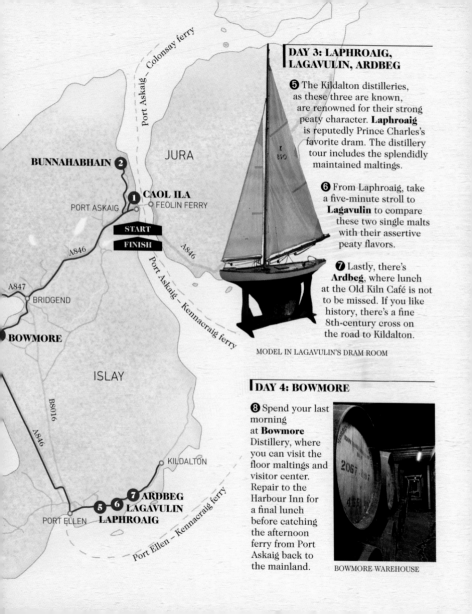

Port Askaig – Colonsay ferry

JURA

BUNNAHABHAIN ❷

❶ CAOL ILA
PORT ASKAIG   FEOLIN FERRY

START

FINISH

Port Askaig – Kennacraig ferry

A846

A846

A847

BRIDGEND

BOWMORE

ISLAY

B8016

A846

KILDALTON

❼ ARDBEG
❺ ❻ LAGAVULIN
LAPHROAIG

PORT ELLEN

Port Ellen – Kennacraig ferry

BRAUNSTEIN

Denmark

Braunstein, Carlsensvej 5, 4600 Koge
www.braunstein.dk

A microbrewery located in an old warehouse in Koge harbor, Braunstein uses a small still to make spirit from malted barley. The resulting spirit is clean, fresh, and fruity. Maturation takes place in ex-Oloroso sherry casks. A new edition of the whisky is added each year. The distillery also manufactures aquavit, herbal spirits, schnapps, and a beer called BB Amber Lager. Tastings are held each month.

◀ **BRAUNSTEIN**
SINGLE MALT (VARIABLE ABV)
Fruits, raisins, and chocolate come to the fore in this single malt that varies in strength from batch to batch.

BRUICHLADDICH

Scotland
Bruichladdich, Isle of Islay
www.bruichladdich.com

Islay's most westerly distillery
stands on the shores of Loch
Indaal, across the water from
Bowmore. Unlike older Islay
distilleries, it was purpose-built in
1881 with state-of-the-art cavity
walls and its own steam generator.

After repeated sales, it was
closed down in 1994, seemingly
for good. Then, days before
Christmas 2000, it was rescued
by a private consortium led by
the independent bottler Murray
McDavid. The old Victorian ☞

BRUICHLADDICH
OCTOMORE 7.1 ▶

SINGLE MALT: ISLAY 59.5% ABV
The nose opens with a hint of peat,
followed by brine and orchard fruits.
The palate is slick, with peat, caramel,
ripe apples, and developing oak.

BRUICHLADDICH
THE SCOTTISH BARLEY

SINGLE MALT: ISLAY 50% ABV
Baked apples and linseed on the nose
after a slightly metallic opening. Rich
fruit notes open the palate, with
vanilla, toffee, and brine.

B

BRUICHLADDICH

decor has been lovingly preserved, and no computers are used in the production. The whisky even uses barley grown on the island.

In 2003 Bruichladdich became the first distillery on Islay to bottle its whiskies on the island. From the heavily sherried Blacker Still and the pink-hued Flirtation, to 3D, Infinity, and The Yellow Submarine, the range of bottlings has been staggering. To date, over 200, many of them in very limited quantities, have been released.

In 2012, Rémy Cointreau acquired the distillery; since then, the number of expressions available has reduced significantly.

◀ BRUICHLADDICH THE CLASSIC LADDIE

SINGLE MALT: ISLAY 46% ABV
Chocolate, icing sugar, and rock salt on the nose, with kiwi fruit on the palate, plus spicy, brine notes.

BRUICHLADDICH ISLAY BARLEY 2009

SINGLE MALT: ISLAY 50% ABV
Vanilla, honey, red apples, and an earthy malt on the nose. Closing with cinnamon and dried fruits.

BUCHANAN'S

Scotland

Owner: Diageo
www.buchananswhisky.com

James Buchanan was one of the most notable whisky barons—the Victorian entrepreneurs who brought Scotch to world attention, amassing personal fortunes along the way. Starting as an agent in 1879, he soon began trading on his own and rapidly saw his whisky adopted in the House of Commons. Today the Buchanan's brand is showing signs of prospering once again under its owners, Diageo. Mainly seen in Venezuela, Mexico, Colombia, and the US, Buchanan's is positioned as a premium-style blend. There are two expressions: a 12-year-old and the Special Reserve at 18 years old.

BUCHANAN'S 12-YEAR-OLD ▶
BLEND 40% ABV
Rich on the nose, with sherry and spice. Thinner on the palate, with bitter, dried-lemon notes. Winey, with a touch of dry wood.

BUFFALO TRACE

US

*Buffalo Trace Distillery,
1001 Wilkinson Boulevard,
Frankfort, Kentucky
www.buffalotrace.com*

Formerly known as Ancient Age
(*see p16*), Buffalo Trace is located
at a crossing point where, in the
past, herds of migrating buffalo
forded the Kentucky River. The
trail they followed was known
as the Great Buffalo Trace.

Buffalo Trace boasts the
broadest age-range of whiskey
in the US (from 4 to 23 years)
and is the only US distillery using
five recipes—a wheat whiskey,
a rye whiskey, two rye bourbons,
and a barley. The Buffalo Trace
Experimental Collection of
cask strength, wine-barrel-aged
whiskeys was launched in 2006.

◀ BUFFALO TRACE KENTUCKY STRAIGHT BOURBON
BOURBON 45% ABV

Aged a minimum of nine years, this
has aromas of vanilla, gum, mint, and
molasses. Sweet, fruity, and spicy on
the palate, with emerging brown sugar
and oak. The finish is long, spicy, and
fairly dry, with developing vanilla.

BULLEIT

US

*Four Roses Distillery,
1224 Bonds Mill Road,
Lawrenceburg, Kentucky
www.bulleit.com*

Bulleit Bourbon originated in the 1830s with tavern-keeper and small-time distiller Augustus Bulleit, but production ceased after his death in 1860. However, the brand was revived, using the original recipe, in 1987 by his great-great-grandson Tom Bulleit. Seagram subsequently took over the label and from there it passed to Diageo. Although it is distilled by Four Roses (*see p121*), brand owner Diageo has created a Bulleit Experience at the silent Stitzel-Weller Distillery in Louisville.

BULLEIT BOURBON ▷

BOURBON 40% ABV
Rich, oaky aromas lead into a mellow flavor, focused around vanilla and honey. The medium-length finish features vanilla and a hint of smoke.

BUNNAHABHAIN

Scotland
Port Askaig, Islay
www.bunnahabhain.com

Before the distilleries found
fame for their heavily peat-smoked
single malts, their market was not
the whisky drinker, but the big
blending houses. The blenders
only required limited quantities
of smoky malt, however, as too
much would leave their whiskies
unbalanced. With this in mind,
Bunnahabhain used unpeated
or lightly peated malt.
Bunnahabhain also produces
limited-edition bottlings for the
Fèis Ìle, Islay's annual festival.

◄ BUNNAHABHAIN 12-YEAR-OLD

SINGLE MALT: ISLAY 40% ABV
A clean, refreshing whisky with
a scent of ozone and sea spray, which
gives way to a nutty malty sweetness
in the mouth.

BUNNAHABHAIN 18-YEAR-OLD

SINGLE MALT: ISLAY 43% ABV
With its richer sherry influence, this
has less of the malty distillery character
than the 12-year-old. Instead it has a
broader texture and woody flavor.

BUSHMILLS

Ireland
*2 Distillery Road, Bushmills,
County Antrim
www.bushmills.com*

Old Bushmills has the amazing
ability to be all things to all
people: a thoroughly modern
distillery housed in a beautiful
Victorian building; a boutique
distillery that nevertheless
produces global brands; and a
working distillery that welcomes
the public.

Bushmills produces only malt
whiskey, so the grain used in its
blends is made to order in the
Midleton Distillery. ☞

BUSHMILLS ORIGINAL ▶
BLEND 40% ABV

A fruity, easy-to-drink, vanilla-infused
mouthfeel. Its clean, clear character
makes it very approachable. A lovely
entry to the world of Irish whiskey.

BUSHMILLS BLACK BUSH
BLEND 40% ABV

A living legend, Black Bush is the
lovable rogue of the family. It is
a very classy glassful of honey-nut
scrumptiousness with an extremely
silky mouthfeel. The benchmark for
Irish blends.

BUSHMILLS

Unusually, Bushmills doesn't have a problem selling single malts and blends under the same brand name: it is a distillery that isn't afraid to push the boundaries. An example of this is the whiskey it produced to celebrate the 400th anniversary of its original licence to distill, a limited edition blended whiskey made using crystal malt—the kind usually found in breweries.

◄ BUSHMILLS MALT 10-YEAR-OLD

SINGLE MALT 40% ABV

A triple-distilled, peat-free whiskey, this charmer appeals to just about everyone. There's a hint of sherry wood, and the malt is sweet with hints of fudgy chocolate. A classic and very approachable Irish malt.

BUSHMILLS MALT 16-YEAR-OLD

SINGLE MALT 40% ABV

This malt isn't just a straight aging of the classic 10-year-old. It's a half-and-half mix of bourbon and sherry cask–matured malt, married for a further nine months in port pipes. The three woods bring their own magic to bear, and produce a riot of dried-fruit flavors cut with almonds and the ever-present honey.

CAMERON BRIG

Scotland

Cameronbridge Distillery, Winygates, Leven, Fife

Greatly misunderstood, little drunk in their own right, and sadly misrepresented, grain whiskies are Scotch's poor relation. Yet, they are the essential component and base of all blends and, when found as a single grain bottling, the source of much pleasure.

Cameron Brig is made at Diageo's Cameronbridge distillery in Fife, a massive complex of giant continuous stills. The sheer scale of grain whisky production offends some purists but, at its best, good grain whisky is very good indeed. You would not expect anything less from Diageo in its only offering in this category, and Cameron Brig won't disappoint.

**CAMERON BRIG
12-YEAR-OLD** ▶

SINGLE GRAIN 40% ABV

The nose is clean and grassy, with some honey. Smooth palate; nutty and firm, with a hint of bitter coffee in the finish.

CANADIAN CLUB

Canada

Hiram Walker Distillery,
Riverside Drive East,
Walkerville, Ontario
www.canadianclub.com

Canadian Club is the oldest and most influential whisky brand in Canada. Created by businessman Hiram Walker in 1884, it was named simply "Club" and aimed at discerning members of gentlemen's clubs. Unusually, in an era when most whiskies were sold in bulk, it was supplied in bottles (and thus could not be adulterated by the retailer), a practice soon adopted by other Canadian and American distillers.

◀ CANADIAN CLUB 1858
BLEND 40% ABV
Floral notes on the nose, with dried fruits and rye. The palate is oily, sweet, fruity, and mildly herbal, with white pepper.

CANADIAN CLUB SMALL BATCH SHERRY CASK
BLEND 41.3% ABV
Rye, pine, freshly sawn timber, ginger, and discreet sweet sherry on the nose, while the palate yields vanilla, caramel, black pepper, and light fruit notes.

The company has had numerous Royal Warrants, from Queen Victoria to Elizabeth II. A less lofty customer, Al Capone, smuggled thousands of cases across the border during Prohibition.

The Canadian Club brands were sold to Fortune Brands, the owner of Jim Beam (see p201), in 2005. Canadian Club is always "blended at birth"—that is, the component whiskies are mixed prior to a maturation of at least five years. The standard is a 6-year-old; older versions, such as the 20-year-old, are sometimes released onto the domestic and export markets.

CANADIAN CLUB RESERVE 9-YEAR-OLD ▶

BLEND 40% ABV

Vanilla, maple syrup, rye, and fresh oak on the nose, while the palate offers spicy rye, butterscotch, and milk chocolate, underpinned by corn notes.

CANADIAN CLUB SMALL BATCH CLASSIC 12

BLEND 40% ABV

Caramel, orange, and hand rolling tobacco on the nose, with cereal, honey, and spice. More caramel and oranges on the gently spiced palate, with almonds and dates.

CANADIAN MIST

Canada

*202 MacDonald Road,
Collingwood, Ontario
www.canadianmist.com*

Launched in 1965, this whisky
now sells 3 million cases a year
in the US. Its distillery is odd in
several ways: the equipment is
all stainless steel; it is the only
Canadian distillery to use a
mashbill of corn and malted
barley; and it imports its rye
spirit from sister distillery Early
Times (*see p111*) in Kentucky.
Almost all the spirit is tankered
to Kentucky for blending. In
addition to the popular Canadian
Mist brand, the 1185 Special
Reserve is also available.

◄ CANADIAN MIST

BLEND 40% ABV

Lightly fruity on the nose, with vanilla
and caramel notes. Mild, sweet flavor
with traces of vanilla toffee.

CAOL ILA

Scotland
Port Askaig, Islay
www.malts.com

For years, Caol Ila played second fiddle to Lagavulin within the Diageo stable. This is beginning to change, as its owners are now promoting Caol Ila as a top-quality single malt.

The distillery was built in 1846, and by 1857 was in the hands of Glasgow blender Bulloch Lade, who reconstructed Caol Ila on a larger scale in 1879.

The distillery was effectively demolished in 1972, re-opening two years later with the warehouse the only part remaining.

CAOL ILA 12-YEAR-OLD ▶
SINGLE MALT: ISLAY 43% ABV
Malty sweetness and citrus aromas balance the scent of tar and peat. Oily textured, with treacly, smoky flavors.

CAOL ILA DISTILLERS EDITION 1995
SINGLE MALT: ISLAY 43% ABV
Sweet, smoky, and malty, with aromatic spices (cinnamon), especially in the lingering finish. The most rounded expression of the core range.

CARDHU

Scotland
Knockando, Aberlour, Morayshire
www.malts.com

Cardhu Distillery was a small farm distillery until Elizabeth Cumming rebuilt it in the 1880s. Soon after, it was sold to Johnnie Walker and became the spiritual home of the blend. In the 1990s, increased demand in Spain for Cardhu 12-year-old led owners Diageo to re-christen the whisky as Cardhu Pure Malt, so they could add other malts and so increase production. But outrage within the industry forced Diageo to withdraw the brand and revert to selling Cardhu as a genuine single malt.

◀ CARDHU 12-YEAR-OLD
SINGLE MALT: SPEYSIDE 40% ABV
A heathery, pear drop–scented malt. Light to medium body; malty, slightly nutty flavor that finishes fairly short.

CARDHU AMBER ROCK
SINGLE MALT: SPEYSIDE 40% ABV
Stewed apples, dried fruit, and icing sugar on the nose. Summer fruits, vanilla, and spice on the palate. Drying oak and licorice in the finish.

CATDADDY

US

Piedmont Distillers,
203 East Murphy Street,
Madison, North Carolina
www.catdaddymoonshine.com

Piedmont is the only licensed
distillery in North Carolina, and
its Catdaddy Moonshine celebrates
the state's great heritage of illicit
distilling. In 2005, ex-New Yorker
Joe Michalek established Piedmont
in Madison. It is the first legal
distillery in the Carolinas since
before Prohibition. "According
to the lore of moonshine, only
the best moonshine earns the
right to be called the Catdaddy,"
says Joe Michalek. "True to the
history of moonshine, every
batch of Catdaddy is born in
an authentic copper pot still."

CATDADDY
CAROLINA MOONSHINE ▶

CORN WHISKEY 40% ABV

Triple-distilled from corn in small
batches, Catdaddy is sweet and spicy,
with notes of vanilla and cinnamon.

CATTO'S

Scotland
Owner: Inver House Distillers

James Catto, an Aberdeen-based whisky blender, set up in business in 1861. His whiskies achieved international distribution on the White Star and P&O shipping lines. After the death of his son Robert in World War I, the company passed to the distillers Gilbey's. More recently, it was acquired by Inver House Distillers. Catto's is a deluxe, fully matured, and complex blend. Two versions are available: a non-age standard bottling and a 12-year-old expression with a yellow-gold, strawlike appearance that belies its complexity and warm finish.

◀ **CATTO'S**

BLEND 40% ABV

The standard Catto blend is aromatic and well-rounded in character, with a smooth, mellow finish.

CHARBAY

US

Domaine Charbay,
4001 Spring Mountain Road,
St. Helena, California
www.charbay.com

The father-and-son partnership of Miles and Marko Karakasevic are 12th- and 13th-generation winemakers and distillers. Charbay whiskeys are distilled in a 1,000-gallon (3,750-liter) copper alembic Charentais pot still. Many innovative whiskeys have emerged from the still, including R5 Lot No. 3, double-distilled from Bear Republic IPA, and Whiskey S (Lot 211A), produced from Bear Republic Stout. Whiskey Release III was distilled using Pilsner.

CHARBAY WHISKEY RELEASE III 6-YEAR-OLD ▶

AMERICAN WHISKEY 66.2% ABV
This "hop-flavored whiskey" offers an herbal, lagerlike nose, with lemon and cloves, plus a note of vanilla. Big fruit, spice, and herbal notes on the full palate, with developing oak.

CHICHIBU

Japan

Venture Whisky, Saitama Prefecture
www.one-drinks.com

The newest Japanese distillery was founded in 2007 by Ichiro Akuto, previously of Hanyu *(see p172)*. A small plant, it features what might be the only Japanese oak washbacks in the world. Aging takes place in a mix of more than 20 cask types, including ex-bourbon, ex-sherry, ex-Madeira, and ex-cognac casks. Some 10 percent of the barley used is malted on site, and batches of peated spirit are distilled annually. Chichibu releases are highly prized and difficult to obtain, even in Japan.

◀ ICHIRO'S MALT CHICHIBU THE PEATED

SINGLE MALT 62.5% ABV

Warm asphalt, earthy peat, lemon, new oak, and sea spray on the nose. The palate is smooth, with sweet peat, new leather, licorice, citrus fruit, and plain chocolate.

CHIVAS REGAL

Scotland
Owner: Chivas Brothers

Chivas Brothers was founded in the early 19th century and prospered, due in part to some favorable royal connections. Chivas is owned today by the French Pernod Ricard.

At the heart of Chivas Regal blends are Speyside single malt whiskies, in particular Strathisla Distillery's rich and full single malt. To safeguard the supply of this critically important ingredient, Chivas Brothers bought the distillery in 1950.

CHIVAS REGAL 25-YEAR-OLD ▶
BLEND 40% ABV
The flagship blend, Chivas Regal 25-year-old is classy and rich. A luxury blend for indulgent sipping. Well-mannered, balanced, and stylish.

CHIVAS REGAL 12-YEAR-OLD
BLEND 40% ABV
An aromatic infusion of wild herbs, heather, honey, and orchard fruits. Round and creamy on the palate, with a full, rich taste of honey and ripe apples and notes of vanilla, hazelnut, and butterscotch. Rich and lingering.

CLAN CAMPBELL

Scotland
Owner: Chivas Brothers

Launched as recently as 1984, Clan Campbell is a million-case-selling brand from Chivas Brothers, the whisky arm of drinks giant Pernod Ricard. It is not available in the UK, but is a leader in the important French market, and may also be found in Italy, Spain, and some Asian countries. Despite its relative youth, its origins are now inextricably entwined with Scottish heritage, thanks to clever marketing and a link to the Duke of Argyll, head of the clan. Indeed, what is claimed to be the oldest whisky-distilling relic in Scotland—a distiller's worm—was luckily found on Campbell lands.

◀ CLAN CAMPBELL
BLEND 40% ABV
The malt component of Clan Campbell comes largely from Speyside (Aberlour and Glenallachie especially). A smooth, light whisky with a fruity finish.

THE CLAYMORE

Scotland
Owner: Whyte & Mackay

A claymore is a Highland
broadsword. The name was
deemed appropriate by DCL
(forerunner of drinks giant Diageo)
when, in 1977, it attempted to
recover some of the market share
it had lost when it withdrew
Johnnie Walker Red Label from
the UK market. Competitively
priced, The Claymore was an
immediate success. In 1985,
the brand was sold to Whyte
& Mackay. It continued to sell
well for some time, but in recent
years has declined and is now
principally seen as a low-priced
secondary brand. Dalmore is
believed to be the main malt
whisky in the blend.

THE CLAYMORE ▶

BLEND 40% ABV
The nose is heavy and full, with
silky mellow tones. Well-balanced
and full-bodied on the palate.
Polished finish.

CLUNY

Scotland
Owner: Whyte & Mackay

Although it is produced by Whyte & Mackay, Cluny is supplied in bulk to Heaven Hill Distilleries, which has bottled the whisky in the US since 1988. Today it is one of America's top-selling domestically bottled, blended Scotch whiskies. It contains over 30 malts from all regions of Scotland (Isle of Jura, Dalmore, and Fettercairn single malts among them), along with grain whisky that is almost certainly largely sourced from Whyte & Mackay's Invergordon plant. Cluny is sold primarily on its competitive price. Under Whyte & Mackay's new Indian ownership, it may be a candidate for further international development.

◄ **CLUNY**
BLEND 40% ABV
Subtle sweet and sour nose, with a slight metallic, bitter tang on the palate.

CLYNELISH

Scotland
Brora, Sutherland
www.malts.com

A large, box-shaped distillery
dating from 1967, Clynelish has
six stills and a capacity of 750,000
gallons (3.4 million liters). Within
its grounds is a much older
distillery that ran alongside it until
1983. This was Brora, founded in
1819 by the Marquis of Stafford.
Known briefly as Old Clynelish,
Brora made a heavily peated malt
during the 1970s to ensure a
supply of Islay-style malts for
blends like Johnnie Walker Black
Label. In 1983 Brora closed for
good, leaving just Clynelish.
There have been various rare
malts and independent bottlings
from Douglas Laing and
Cadenhead, among others.

CLYNELISH 14-YEAR-OLD ▶
SINGLE MALT: HIGHLANDS 46% ABV
A mouthfilling malt, quite fruity with
a creamy texture, a wisp of smoke, and
a firm, dry finish.

COLERAINE

Ireland
*Coleraine Distillery Ltd.,
Hawthorn Office Park,
Stockman's Way, Belfast*

Never underestimate the selling power of nostalgia: the sole reason this blend is still produced is because whiskey drinkers are very brand loyal, and the name Coleraine still has resonance some three decades after the distillery fell silent. It once produced a single malt of some repute, then in 1954 it started to make grain whiskey for Bushmills, before it was eventually wound down in the 1970s. The reputation of the distillery was such, however, that customers still look out for the name, and so a brand and blend were created to fill a niche. Although the company is called Coleraine Distillery, the whiskey is produced elsewhere.

◀ COLERAINE

BLEND 40% ABV

Light, sweet, and grainy. Probably best suited to drinking with a mixer.

COMPASS BOX

Scotland
www.compassboxwhisky.com

Compass Box was formed in
2000 and describes itself as an
"artisanal whisky maker," which
may seem disingenuous since
it isn't a distiller but a blender,
albeit a highly innovative one. Its
technique of inserting additional
oak staves into a barrel to produce
Spice Tree led to pressure from
the Scotch Whisky Association
and the eventual withdrawal of the
product. For all this, the company
has been highly influential, and in
its short life has won more than
60 medals and awards.

COMPASS BOX
THE PEAT MONSTER ▶

BLENDED MALT:
ISLAY / SPEYSIDE 46% ABV
Rich and loaded with flavor:
a bacon-fat smokiness, full-blown
peat, hints of fruit and spice. A long
finish, echoing peat and smoke.

COMPASS BOX ASYLA

BLEND 40% ABV
A frequent award-winner. Sweet,
delicate, and very smooth on the
palate. Flavors of vanilla cream,
cereals, and a subtle apple character.

The PEAT
MONSTER
MALT SCOTCH WHISKY
*Big, Peaty, Smoky. A superb, balanced
and delicious combination of smoky, peaty Islay
malt whisky with rich, old Speyside malt.*
-John Glaser, Whiskymaker.

COMPASS BOX
WHISKY COMPANY

CONNEMARA

Ireland

Cooley Distillery, Riverstown,
Cooley, County Louth
www.kilbeggandistillingcompany.com

In the eyes of the Irish whiskey industry—and many a traditionalist as well—Irish whiskey was a triple-distilled and unpeated drink. Then along came Cooley's John Teeling, who started making Irish whiskey that was double-distilled and peated. It caused quite a stir. Yet Connemara has gone from being a curiosity to winning gold medals. In December 2011, Beam Inc. acquired Cooley from the Teeling family, and early in 2014, Suntory took over Beam, creating Beam Suntory Inc. Several expressions of Connemara have been offered, but today, only the flagship Original variant is produced.

◀ CONNEMARA ORIGINAL

SINGLE MALT 40% ABV

A smoldering turf fire on the nose, with marshmallows, honey, and floral notes. Spicy malt, sweet smoke, and peppery, drying oak on the palate.

CRAGGANMORE

Scotland

Ballindalloch, Morayshire
www.malts.com

This was a well-conceived distillery from the start. Built in 1869, it had a reliable source of pure water from the Craggan burn, nearby access to peat and barley, and its proximity to Ballindalloch station enabled it to become the first distillery in Scotland to have its own railway siding, to bring in supplies and carry off the freshly filled casks. Unusual flat-topped stills and worm tubs may add to Cragganmore's famed complexity.

CRAGGANMORE 12-YEAR-OLD ▶

SINGLE MALT: SPEYSIDE 40% ABV
Floral, heathery aromas, then a robust, woody complexity with a trace of smoke on the palate.

CRAGGANMORE DISTILLERS EDITION 1992

SINGLE MALT: SPEYSIDE 43% ABV
Double-matured, including a spell in a port cask, there is a cherry and orange sweetness that dies away into a lightly smoky finish.

CRAIGELLACHIE

Scotland
Craigellachie, Banffshire
www.craigellachie.com

Although the name of John Dewar & Sons is writ large above the modern, plate-glass stillhouse that sits on the main road out of Craigellachie, the distillery was originally tied to White Horse. Peter Mackie, the man behind the famous blend, built Craigellachie in 1891 in partnership with Alexander Edward. Of all the Victorian whisky barons, Mackie was the most connected to malt distilling, having served as an apprentice at Lagavulin, whose whisky was also part of White Horse. Since 1998, Craigellachie has been owned by Bacardi.

◄ CRAIGELLACHIE 13-YEAR-OLD
SINGLE MALT: SPEYSIDE 46% ABV
The nose is fresh and fruity, with just a hint of spent matches and a nutty, savory note. Oily and sweet on the early palate, with more savory notes coming through in time, plus a hint of charcoal.

CRAOI NA MÓNA

Ireland

Cooley Distillery, Riverstown,
Cooley, County Louth
Owner: Berry Bros. & Rudd

Craoi na móna is Gaelic for "heart of peat." Produced by Cooley, though not one of its own brands, this whiskey can be found in places as diverse as Moscow and London, but so far it hasn't been spotted in Dublin. Given the huge rise in the popularity of Irish whiskey recently, it's not surprising that so many drinks companies are trying to cut themselves a slice of the action. The Craoi na Móna brand is owned by leading London wine merchants Berry Bros. & Rudd, and at 10 years of age, is part of their Berrys' Own Selection range.

CRAOI NA MÓNA ▶

SINGLE MALT 40% ABV
Sweet and young, this is a decidedly immature peated malt.

CRAWFORD'S

Scotland

Owner: Whyte & Mackay / Diageo

Crawford's 3 Star was established by Leith firm A. & A. Crawford, and by the time the company joined the Distillers Company (DCL) in 1944, the blend was a Scottish favorite. Although its popularity continued, it was not of strategic significance to its owners, hence the decision to license the brand to Whyte & Mackay in 1986. Whyte & Mackay are today owned by the Indian UB Group, so the future of this venerable label may lie on the subcontinent. Diageo, successors to DCL, retain the rights to the name Crawford's 3 Star Special Reserve outside the UK. Benrinnes single malt (*see p45*) has been a longtime component in the Crawford's blend.

◀ CRAWFORD'S 3 STAR SPECIAL RESERVE

BLEND 40% ABV

A spirity, fruity, fresh-tasting blend, with a smack of citrus, a sweet center, and a dry, slightly sooty finish.

CROWN ROYAL

Canada
Distillery Road, Gimli, Manitoba
www.crownroyal.ca

Crown Royal was created by Sam Bronfman, President of Seagram (*see p310*), to mark the state visit to Canada of King George VI and Queen Elizabeth in 1939, with its "crown-shaped" bottle and purple velvet bag. Although it was only available in Canada until 1964, it is now one of the best-selling Canadian whiskies in the US.

Since 1992, it has been produced at the Gimli Distillery on Lake Winnipeg. In 2001 Seagram's shed its alcohol interests and both Gimli Distillery and the Crown Royal brand went to Diageo.

CROWN ROYAL DELUXE ▶
BLEND 40% ABV
Nose of toffee, vanilla, and cereal. Smooth palate of caramel, peaches, and oak.

CROWN ROYAL BLACK
BLEND 45% ABV
Rum and raisin ice cream sprinkled with black pepper on the nose, while vanilla, caramel, and oak dominate the fruity palate.

CUTTY SARK

Scotland
Owner: Berry Bros. & Rudd

Blended and bottled in Glasgow by Edrington, Cutty Sark was created in 1923 for Berry Bros. & Rudd Ltd., a well-established London wine and spirit merchant who is still the brand owner.

The first very pale-colored whisky in the world, Cutty Sark uses some 20 single malt whiskies, many from Speyside distilleries such as Glenrothes and Macallan. The wood for the oak casks is carefully chosen to bring out the characteristic flavor and aroma of each whisky in the Cutty Sark blend and to impart color gently during the long maturation.

◀ CUTTY SARK ORIGINAL
BLEND 40% ABV

Light and fragrant aroma, with hints of vanilla and oak. Sweet and creamy, with a vanilla note, and a crisp finish.

CUTTY SARK 12-YEAR-OLD
BLEND 43% ABV

Elegant and fruity, with a subtle vanilla sweetness. Here the malts used are between 12 and 15 years old.

DAILUAINE

Scotland
Carron, Banffshire
www.malts.com

Under the shadow of Benrinnes, a local farmer called William Mackenzie built Dailuaine in 1854. His son Thomas later went into partnership with James Fleming to form Dailuaine-Talisker Distilleries Ltd. In 1889 Dailuaine was rebuilt and became one of the biggest distilleries in Scotland. The architect Charles Doig erected his first pagoda roof here, to draw smoke from the kiln through the malt. The idea caught on at other distilleries. With all but 2 percent of Dailuaine used as fillings, single malt bottlings are relatively rare.

DAILUAINE GORDON & MACPHAIL 1993 ▶
SINGLE MALT: SPEYSIDE 43% ABV
Sweet and malty, with spicy notes of licorice and aniseed. Oaky, toasty notes, too. Creamier with a little water.

DALLAS DHU

Scotland
Forres, Morayshire

This late-Victorian distillery, founded in 1898 by the Master Distiller Alexander Edward, was one of many owned by the Distillers Company Limited (DCL) to be shut down in 1983 to await its fate. With just two stills and a waterwheel that had provided the power for the distillery right up until 1971, Dallas Dhu never fully embraced the 20th century. However, while its stills have never been fired up again, it has lived on as a museum run by Historic Scotland. Thousands of visitors have taken the tour and tried a drop of the malt in a blend called Roderick Dhu. Rumors of its restart persist.

◄ DALLAS DHU RARE MALTS 21-YEAR-OLD

SINGLE MALT: SPEYSIDE 61.9% ABV
Full-bodied, almost Highland character on the nose, with a trace of smoke and a robust, malty flavor.

96

THE DALMORE

Scotland
Alness, Ross-shire
www.thedalmore.com

While the Whyte & Mackay blend has a long association with Glasgow, its heart lies in the Highlands, in Dalmore on the banks of the Cromarty Firth. The distillery became part of Whyte & Mackay in 1960, and The Dalmore is now the company's flagship single malt.

The name Dalmore is a fusion of Norse and Gaelic and means "the big meadowland." The distillery stands facing the Black Isle, where some of Scotland's best barley is grown. With ample supplies of ☞

THE DALMORE 12-YEAR-OLD ▶
SINGLE MALT: HIGHLANDS 40% ABV
The well-established 12-year-old has a gentle flavor of candied peel and vanilla fudge.

THE DALMORE 1974
SINGLE MALT: HIGHLANDS 45% ABV
Smooth and full-bodied, with sherry notes, bananas, dark chocolate orange, coffee, walnuts, and a long finish.

97

THE DALMORE

 grain, plenty of local peat, and water from the Alness River, the site was well-chosen.

For years, the only distillery bottling of Dalmore was a 12-year-old single malt, but in time a 21- and 30-year-old were added, along with Gran Reserva (formerly known as the Cigar Malt) in 2002. That year also saw a 62-year-old expression bought at auction for a record-breaking $38,816. Since then, the core range has swelled alongside limited-release bottlings. Many of these have played on different cask maturation, a subject that clearly fascinates Whyte & Mackay's Master Blender, Richard Paterson.

◀ THE DALMORE 15-YEAR-OLD
SINGLE MALT: HIGHLANDS 40% ABV
This has the characteristic rich, fruity sherry influence, but with rather more spice—cloves, cinnamon, and ginger.

THE DALMORE 40-YEAR-OLD
SINGLE MALT: HIGHLANDS 40% ABV
After years in American oak casks, this Dalmore was poured into second-fill Matusalem Oloroso sherry butts and then Amoroso sherry wood.

DALWHINNIE

Scotland
Dalwhinnie, Inverness-shire
www.malts.com

Founded in 1897, Dalwhinnie
used to claim to be the highest
distillery in Scotland, at 1,073 ft
(327 m) above sea level, but it has
since been eclipsed by Braeval.
Its other claim to fame holds good,
however: with a mean annual
temperature of just 43°F (6°C),
Dalwhinnie remains the coldest
distillery in the country. In 1905
it became Scotland's first
American-owned distillery,
bought by the New York company
Cook & Bernheimer, and the
Stars and Stripes were raised
above the owners' warehouse in
Leith. Since 1926 it has been part
of DCL (now Diageo), supplying
blends such as Black & White.

DALWHINNIE 15-YEAR-OLD ▶
SINGLE MALT: HIGHLANDS 43% ABV
Sweet, aromatic, and subtly infused
with smoke, this complex malt is thick
on the tongue.

DEANSTON

Scotland

Deanston, Perthshire
www.deanstonmalt.com

Many distilleries evolved from illicit stills on the farm, others from breweries or malt mills, but only Deanston is a former cotton mill. It was founded in 1785 by Richard Arkwright, one of the great pioneers of the Industrial Revolution. The conversion to whisky-making took place in 1965, in a joint venture with Brodie Hepburn, who also owned Tullibardine. Deanston was soon producing a single malt—Old Bannockburn was released in 1971. Having spent most of the 1980s in mothballs, the distillery was bought by Burn Stewart, now owned by South African Distell Group, in 1990.

◀ DEANSTON 12-YEAR-OLD

SINGLE MALT: HIGHLANDS 40% ABV
Non–chill filtered and relatively light-bodied, it has a nutty, vanilla flavor.

DEWAR'S

Scotland
www.dewars.com

When it was bought by Bacardi in 1988, the whole Dewar's enterprise was reinvigorated. The brand was repackaged, with much investment made throughout the business, from distilling to bottling. New products were developed to augment the standard White Label—one of the biggest-selling Scotch blends in the US. First of these was a 12-year-old expression, Special Reserve, followed by the 18-year-old Founder's Reserve bottling, and finally an ultra-premium non-age style known as Signature. ☞

DEWAR'S 12-YEAR-OLD ▶
BLEND 40% ABV
Sweetish and floral. A full and rich blend, with honey and caramel, and licorice notes in the long finish.

DEWAR'S WHITE LABEL
BLEND 40% ABV
Sweet and heathery on the nose. Medium-bodied, fresh, malty, and vaguely spicy, with a clean, slightly dry finish.

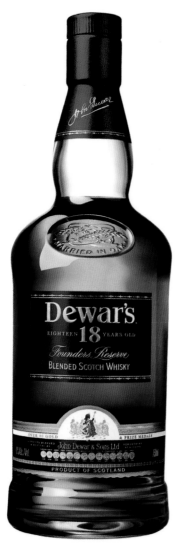

DEWAR'S

🍂 The main single malt in the
Dewar's blends is Aberfeldy,
although the group's other single
malts—Aultmore, Craigellachie,
Royal Brackla, and MacDuff—
are also used.

Dewar's is not widely available
in the UK, but is dominant in the
US. It is also important in parts of
Europe and is gaining a following
in Asia. Bacardi has expanded
global distribution for Dewar's
and greatly expanded its profile
through increased advertising
and marketing. Standards of
production have been kept high,
and some would say that the blend
quality has improved, especially
in the new products.

◀ DEWAR'S 18-YEAR-OLD
BLEND 43% ABV
Here the Dewar's nose is more
delicately perfumed, with notes of pear
and lemon zest. Soft on the palate, but
drying, with a slightly spicy finish.

DEWAR'S SIGNATURE
BLEND 43% ABV
A limited-edition blend, with a heavy
share of old Aberfeldy malt. Silky
textured and mellow, with rich fruit
and dark honey to the fore.

DIMPLE / PINCH

Scotland
Owner: Diageo

Launched to marked success in 1890, Haig's Dimple brand, known as Pinch in the US, is today part of the Diageo stable. It has always been a deluxe blend, noted for its distinctive packaging introduced by G. O. Haig in the 1890s. It stood out in particular for the wire net over the bottle, originally applied by hand and intended to prevent the cork from popping out in warm climates or during sea transport. It was the first bottle of its type to be registered as a trademark in the United States, although this was done as late as 1958.

DIMPLE 12-YEAR-OLD ▶
BLEND 40% ABV

Aromas of fudge, with woody notes. Hints of mint, and an initial richness on the palate, with candy apples and caramel; spiciness and dried fruits, too.

DIMPLE 15-YEAR-OLD
BLEND 43% ABV

In this blend, there are hints of smoke, chocolate, and cocoa, completed by a long, rich finish.

DUFFTOWN

Scotland

Dufftown, Keith, Banffshire
www.malts.com

This epicenter of Speyside whisky-making was bound to have a distillery named after it, although it took until 1896, by which point there were already five distilleries in town. Within a year, Dufftown was owned outright by Peter Mackenzie, who also owned Blair Athol. He was soon selling whisky to the blender Arthur Bell & Sons, who eventually bought Dufftown in 1933. Now part of Diageo, Dufftown continues to supply malt for the Bell's blend and, until recently, had produced little in the way of its own single malt.

◀ **SINGLETON OF DUFFTOWN**

SINGLE MALT: SPEYSIDE 40% ABV
A sweet and eminently drinkable introductory malt. If this recently launched 12-year-old takes off, there should be plenty available—it comes from one of Diageo's biggest distilleries.

DUNGOURNEY 1964

Ireland
Midleton Distillery, Midleton, County Cork

No one is quite sure how, but for 30 years, some of the last pot still to be produced at the old Midleton Distillery lay undiscovered in the corner of a warehouse at Dungourney. In 1994 the remarkable survivor was bottled and named after the river it had come from some three decades before. Dungourney 1964 is a time machine: one sniff and you are transported back to the days when Jameson, Powers, and Paddy came from competing distilleries.

DUNGOURNEY 1964 ▶

IRISH POT STILL WHISKEY 40% ABV
The mushroom edge to the nose gives a hint of age, but the body is still firm. They made whiskey differently back then, which is why this tastes slightly oily, but the tell-tale, almost minty, kick of pure pot still whiskey is still evident.

DUNVILLE'S

Ireland

*Echlinville Distillery, Kircubbin,
County Down*
www.echlinville.com

Echlinville became the first new
Northern Irish distillery in over
125 years when it opened in 2013.
The plan is to produce spirit for
use in the Feckin Irish Whiskey
blends, founded by distillery
owner Shane Braniff, who has also
revived the old Dunville's brand.
At one time, Dunville's Royal
Irish Distillery was the biggest
in Belfast, but Dunville & Co
went into liquidation in 1936.

◄ DUNVILLE'S VERY RARE 10-YEAR-OLD

SINGLE MALT 46% ABV
Finished in Pedro Ximénez sherry
casks, this expression has cut grass,
orchard fruits, and vanilla on the nose,
with a soft, sweet, lightly spiced palate.

DYC

Spain

Beam Global España SA, Pasaje Molino del Arco, 40194 Palazuelos de Eresma, Segovia
www.dyc.es

The first whiskey distillery in Spain was founded in 1959 close to Segovia. It stands next to the Eresma River, famous for the excellent quality of its water.

DYC (which stands for Destilerías y Crianza del Whisky) comes in three versions. The Fine Blend and the 8-year-old are both blends of various grains. The Pure Malt is a blended malt. American oak is used for maturation.

DYC 8-YEAR-OLD ▶
BLEND 40% ABV

Floral, spicy, smoky, grassy, with a hint of honey and heather. Smooth, creamy mouthfeel; malty with hints of vanilla, marzipan, apple, and citrus. A bittersweet, long, smooth finish.

DYC PURE MALT
BLENDED MALT 40% ABV

Fragrant bouquet with hints of citrus, sweetness, honey, and vanilla. Full-bodied, rich malt flavor. The finish is long, sophisticated, and subtle, with hints of heather, honey, and fruit.

EAGLE RARE

US

Buffalo Trace Distillery,
1001 Wilkinson Boulevard,
Frankfort, Kentucky
www.eaglerare.com

The Eagle Rare brand was introduced in 1975 by Canadian distilling giant Joseph E. Seagram & Sons Inc. In 1989 it was acquired by the Sazerac Company of New Orleans. In its present incarnation, Eagle Rare is part of Sazerac's Buffalo Trace Antique Collection, which is updated annually. In addition to the popular 10-year-old expression, Eagle Rare also releases small quantities of a 17-year-old variant in the autumn of each year.

◀ EAGLE RARE 10-YEAR-OLD

BOURBON 45% ABV
Stewed fruits, spicy oak, new leather, brittle toffee, and orange on the nose. Rounded on the palate, with dried fruits, spicy cocoa, almonds, and a lengthy finish.

EARLY TIMES

US

Brown-Forman Distillery,
850 Dixie Highway,
Louisville, Kentucky
www.brown-forman.com

Early Times takes its name from a settlement near Bardstown where it was created in 1860. It cannot be classified as a bourbon because some spirit is put into used barrels, and bourbon legislation dictates that all spirit of that name must be matured in new barrels.

This version of Early Times was introduced in 1981 to compete with the increasingly popular, lighter-bodied Canadian whiskies. The Early Times mashbill is made up of 79 percent corn, 11 percent rye, and 10 percent malted barley.

EARLY TIMES ▶

KENTUCKY WHISKY 40% ABV
Quite light on the nose, with nuts and spices. The palate offers more of the same, along with honey and butterscotch notes, leading into a medium-length finish.

EDDU

France

Des Menhirs, Pont Menhir,
29700 Plomelin, Bretagne
www.distillerie.bzh

The Des Menhirs Distillery started as a manufacturer of apple cider in 1986, but in 1998 ventured into whisky. Most fruit distillers that go into whiskey-making use their existing equipment to distill it on the side. Not so Des Menhirs, which built a separate still just for the production of whisky, which it distills not from barley but from buckwheat (*eddu* in Breton).

◀ EDDU SILVER

BUCKWHEAT WHISKY 40% ABV

Aromatic rose and heather on the nose. Fruity, with a touch of honey, marmalade, and some nutmeg. Velvety body, with vanilla and oak in the finish.

EDDU GREY ROCK

BLEND 40% ABV

A blended variety containing 30 percent buckwheat. Orange and apricot flavors combine with broom flower. A faint sea breeze is framed by a hint of cinnamon. Balanced flavors and a long, long finish.

EDGEFIELD

US

2126 Southwest Halsey Street,
Troutdale, Oregon
www.mcmenamins.com

Operated by the McMenamin's hotel and pub group, Edgefield Distillery is located in a former dry store for root vegetables on the beautiful Edgefield Manor Estate at Troutdale. The distillery has been in production since February 1998 and features a 12-ft (4-m) tall copper and stainless-steel still. According to McMenamin's, it resembles a hybrid of a 19th-century diving suit and oversize coffee urn, a design made famous by Holstein of Germany, the world's oldest surviving still manufacturer.

EDGEFIELD HOGSHEAD ▶

OREGON WHISKEY 46% ABV
Hogshead whiskey has banana and malt on the sweet, floral nose, with vanilla and caramel notes on the palate, plus barley, honey, and oak in the medium-length finish.

EDRADOUR

Scotland
Pitlochry, Perthshire
www.edradour.com

With an output of just 21,000 gallons (95,000 liters) of pure alcohol a year, this picturesque distillery would have been one of many farm distilleries in the Perthshire hills when it was founded in 1825. Today it feels much more special, and a world apart from the large-scale malt distilleries of Speyside. It became part of Pernod Ricard in 1975 but, as the French group expanded to become a huge global player in the whiskey industry, tiny Edradour began to look increasingly out of place. In 2002 it was finally sold to Andrew Symington, owner of independent bottler Signatory.

◀ **EDRADOUR 10-YEAR-OLD**
SINGLE MALT: HIGHLANDS 40% ABV
Clean peppermint nose, with a trace of smoke. Richer, nutty flavors and a silky texture on the tongue.

ELIJAH CRAIG

US

Heaven Hill Distillery,
1701 West Breckinridge Street,
Louisville, Kentucky
www.heavenhill.com

The Reverend Elijah Craig (1743–1808) was a Baptist minister who is widely viewed as the "father of bourbon," having reputedly invented the concept of using charred barrels to store and mature the spirit he made. There seems to be no hard evidence that he was the first person to make bourbon, but the association between a "man of God" and whiskey was seen as a useful tool in the struggle against the temperance movement.

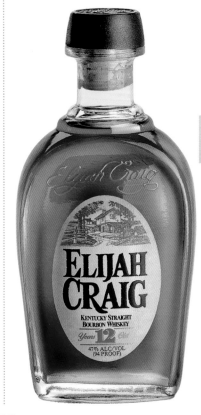

ELIJAH CRAIG 12-YEAR-OLD ▶

BOURBON 47% ABV

A classic bourbon, with aromas of caramel, vanilla, spice, and honey, plus a bit of mint. Full-bodied, rounded on the mellow palate, with caramel, malt, corn, rye, and a little smoke. Sweet oak, licorice, and vanilla dominate the finish.

ELMER T. LEE

US
*Buffalo Trace Distillery,
1001 Wilkinson Boulevard,
Frankfort, Kentucky
www.buffalotrace.com*

Elmer T. Lee is a former Master Distiller at Buffalo Trace (*see p66*), having joined what was then the George T. Stagg Distillery in the 1940s. During his time there, the name changed first to the Albert B. Blanton Distillery (1953), then to the Ancient Age Distillery (1962), and finally to the Buffalo Trace Distillery in 2001. Lee is credited with creating the first modern single barrel bourbon in 1984.

◄ **ELMER T. LEE SINGLE BARREL**
BOURBON 45% ABV
Aged from six to eight years, this expression offers citrus, vanilla, and corn merging on the fragrant nose, with a full and sweet palate, where honey, lingering caramel, and cocoa notes are also evident.

THE ENGLISH WHISKY CO.

England

*St. George's Distillery,
Harling Road, Roudham, Norfolk
www.englishwhisky.co.uk*

England had at least four
distilleries in the 1800s. Sadly,
these had all gone by the turn
of the 20th century, but in 2006,
pot stills produced malt spirit in
England again, thanks to The
English Whisky Co., which hired
distilling legend Iain Henderson
to set things up. Since then,
whisky has been released in
sequential chapters, in both
unpeated and peated formats,
while mainstream Classic and Peated
expressions are also available.

THE ENGLISH WHISKY CO.
CHAPTER 14 ▶
SINGLE MALT 46% ABV
The nose is floral and fruity, with
honey, vanilla, and orange. Oily on
the palate and a lengthy, drying finish.

THE ENGLISH WHISKY CO.
CHAPTER 15
SINGLE MALT 46% ABV
Bonfire and citrus notes on the nose,
with vanilla, more citrus, and chili on
the palate, leading into a dry, oaky finish.

EVAN WILLIAMS

US

Heaven Hill Distillery,
1701 West Breckinridge Street,
Louisville, Kentucky
www.heaven-hill.com

The second biggest-selling bourbon after Jim Beam, Evan Williams takes its name from the person thought by many experts to be Kentucky's first distiller.

Evan Williams was born in Wales but emigrated to Virginia, moving to what would become Kentucky in around 1780. He set up a distillery at the foot of what is now Fifth Street in Louisville.

◀ EVAN WILLIAMS BLACK LABEL

BOURBON 43% ABV

Aromatic, with vanilla and mint notes. The palate is initially sweet, with caramel, malt, and developing leather and spice notes.

EVAN WILLIAMS SINGLE BARREL 1998 VINTAGE

BOURBON 43.3% ABV

Aromatic nose of cereal, dried fruit, caramel, and vanilla. Maple, molasses, cinnamon, nutmeg, and berry notes on the palate. Then a whiff of smoke, plus almonds and honey in the spicy finish.

THE FAMOUS GROUSE

Scotland
Owner: Edrington
www.thefamousgrouse.com

The best-selling blend in Scotland
was created by the Victorian
entrepreneur Matthew Gloag in
1896. At first, it was known
simply as The Grouse Brand, but
it evolved to become The Famous
Grouse. The company was passed
down through the generations
until 1970, when death duties
forced the family to sell to ☛

THE FAMOUS GROUSE
MELLOW GOLD ▶
BLEND 40% ABV
Subtle sherry, vanilla, almonds, and
dried fruits on the nose. Vanilla, brittle
toffee, golden raisins, figs, and mildly
spicy sherry on the palate, which
closes with Jaffa oranges and ginger.

THE FAMOUS GROUSE
ORIGINAL
BLEND 40% ABV
Oak and sherry on the nose, well
balanced with a citrus note. Easy-going,
and full of bright Speyside fruit. Clean
and medium-dry finish.

THE FAMOUS GROUSE

🥃 Highland Distillers, today part of Edrington, which also owns some of Scotland's finest single malt distilleries—Highland Park, Macallan, and Glenrothes among them. Naturally, there are high proportions of these whiskies in The Famous Grouse blend.

The last decade has seen a number of interesting innovations, including The Black Grouse, now rebranded as "Smoky Black." It contains more strongly flavored Islay malt in the blend. Snow Grouse is a grain whisky, sold initially in duty-free outlets. The company recommends it be drunk cold from the freezer, like vodka. A creamy mouth-coating effect results.

◀ THE FAMOUS GROUSE SMOKY BLACK

BLEND 40% ABV

Cream teas, peaches, apples, and jammy aromas. Soft peat and smoke notes on the palate (more so with water), plus vanilla, pepper, and spices, then a gentle finish.

FETTERCAIRN

Scotland

Fettercairn, Laurencekirk, Kincardineshire

While the northeastern flank of the Grampians is full of distilleries spilling down to the Spey, the southern slopes are now depleted. Fettercairn stands as their sole survivor. The distillery was established in 1824 as a farm distillery on the Fasque Estate, which was soon bought by Sir John Gladstone, father of the Victorian prime minister William Gladstone. It remained in family hands until 1939, but since then it has been bought, sold, and mothballed several times. Today Fettercairn is part of Whyte & Mackay, but their main priorities are in the shape of Dalmore and Jura.

FETTERCAIRN FIOR ▶
SINGLE MALT: HIGHLANDS 42% ABV
Weighty, smoky nose of sherry, ginger, orange, and toffee. Palate has smoke, treacle, orange, chocolate, and nuts.

F

FORTY CREEK

Canada
*Kittling Ridge Distillery,
Grimsby, Ontario*
www.fortycreekwhisky.com

Kittling Ridge was named 2008
Canadian Distillery of the Year
by *Whisky Magazine*. Unusually,
it uses pot stills as well as column
stills, and a mashbill of rye, barley,
and corn. Built in 1970, it is part
of a winery and was originally
designed to make *eau de vie*.
John Hall, its owner since 1992,
brings the skills of a winemaker
to distilling: "I am not so bound
by tradition as inspired by it."
Whiskey critic Michael Jackson
called Forty Creek "the most
revolutionary whisky in Canada."

◀ BARREL SELECT
BLEND 40% ABV
A complex, fragrant nose, with soft
fruit, honeysuckle, vanilla, and spice.
A similar palate, with traces of nuts
and leather, and a smooth finish with
lingering fruit and vanilla.

FOUR ROSES

US

1224 Bond Mills Road,
Lawrenceburg, Kentucky
www.fourrosesbourbon.com

Built to a striking Spanish
Mission–style design in 1910,
Four Roses Distillery near
Lawrenceburg takes its name from
the brand first trademarked by
Georgia-born Paul Jones, Jr. in
1888. Legend has it that the
southern belle with whom he was
in love wore a corsage of four red
roses to signify her acceptance of
his marriage proposal, hence the
name he gave to his bourbon.

FOUR ROSES SMALL BATCH ▶
BOURBON 45% ABV
Mild and refined on the nose, with
nutmeg and restrained honey. Bold
and rich on the well-balanced palate,
with spices, fruit, and honey flavors.
The finish is long and insinuating,
with developing notes of vanilla.

FOUR ROSES SINGLE BARREL
BOURBON (VARIABLE ABV)
A rich, complex nose comprising
malt, fruits, spices, and fudge. Long
and mellow in the mouth, with vanilla,
oak, and a hint of menthol. The finish
is long, spicy, and decidedly mellow.

FRYSK HYNDER

The Netherlands

*Us Heit distillery, Snekerstraat 43,
8701 XC Bolsward, Friesland
www.usheitdistillery.nl*

Us Heit (Frisian for "Our Father")
was founded as a brewery in
1970. In 2002, owner Aart van
der Linde, a whiskey enthusiast,
decided to start distilling whisky
with barley from a local mill. It is
the same barley from which Us
Heit beer is made and it is malted
at the distillery. A 3-year-old single
malt, Frysk Hynder, has been
released in limited quantities
every year since 2005. Us Heit
uses different types of cask for
maturing, from ex-bourbon barrels
to wine casks and sherry butts.

◀ **FRYSK HYNDER
SHERRY MATURED**

SINGLE MALT 43% ABV
Sweetish and remarkably soft for a
young whisky. Tasty, with a beautiful
full body and distinct sherry notes.

GARRISON BROTHERS

US

Garrison Brothers Distillery,
1827 Hye Albert Road, Hye, Texas
www.garrisonbros.com

The oldest legal distillery in Texas, Garrison Brothers has produced nothing but bourbon since it opened in 2005. The distillery uses organic yellow corn from the Texas Panhandle, organic winter wheat from the Garrison ranch, and two-row winter barley from the Pacific Northwest and Canada. Grain is ground daily, and the sweet mash is cooked one batch at a time. The distillery receives many visitors, and its whiskey has won several major awards.

GARRISON BROTHERS
TEXAS STRAIGHT BOURBON ▶

BOURBON 47% ABV

Rich aromas of honey and vanilla on the nose, continuing onto the palate of apple, cinnamon, and black pepper.

GEORGE DICKEL

US

*1950 Cascade Hollow Road,
Normandy, Tennessee*
www.georgedickel.com

Along with Jack Daniel's, George Dickel is the last licensed, full-scale distillery in Tennessee, though there were around 700 operating there a century ago.

The Dickel operation was moved to Kentucky after Prohibition arrived in Tennessee in 1910, but later returned to a new distillery close to the original location.

◀ GEORGE DICKEL NO. 12

TENNESSEE WHISKEY 45% ABV
Aromatic, with fruit, leather, butterscotch, and a whiff of charcoal and vanilla. Rich palate with rye, chocolate, fruit, and vanilla. The finish offers vanilla toffee and drying oak.

GEORGE DICKEL BARREL SELECT

TENNESSEE WHISKEY 43% ABV
Aromas of corn, honey, nuts, and caramel lead into a full body with soft vanilla, spices, and roast nuts. A long, creamy finish has almond and spices.

GEORGE T. STAGG

US

Buffalo Trace Distillery,
1001 Wilkinson Boulevard,
Frankfort, Kentucky
www.buffalotracedistillery.com

Part of the Buffalo Trace Antique Collection, George T. Stagg takes its name from the one-time owner of what is now the Buffalo Trace Distillery. In the early 1880s, the distillery was owned by Edmund Haynes Taylor, Jr. During tough economic times, he obtained a loan from his friend Stagg—who later foreclosed on Taylor, taking over his company in the process.

GEORGE T. STAGG
2008 EDITION ▶

BOURBON 72.4% ABV

Distilled in the spring of 1993, this high-strength whiskey boasts a rich nose of butterscotch, marzipan, sweet oak, and cherries. The palate features corn, coffee beans, leather, spice, and oak, with a long toffee and spice finish.

125

GEORGIA MOON

US

Heaven Hill Distillery,
1701 West Breckinridge Street,
Louisville, Kentucky
www.heaven-hill.com

Corn whiskey is distilled from a fermented mash of not less than 80 percent corn, and no minimum maturation period is specified. One of the best-known examples is Heaven Hill's Georgia Moon. With a label that promises that the contents be fewer than 30 days old, and available bottled in a mason jar, Georgia Moon harks back to the old days of moonshining.

◄ GEORGIA MOON

CORN WHISKEY 40% ABV

The nose commences with an initial tang of sour liquor, followed by the smell of sweet corn. The palate suggests cabbage water and plums, along with emerging sweeter, candy-corn notes. The finish is short. Drinkers should not expect anything sophisticated.

GIRVAN

Scotland

*Grangestone Industrial Estate,
Girvan, Ayrshire*

The distillery at Girvan was
established in 1964 by William
Grant & Sons in response to a
perceived threat to their grain-
whisky supplies. Today it includes
a grain-whisky distilling complex,
a gin distillery, and the recently
opened Ailsa Bay single malt
distillery. Until 2013, Girvan
was rarely bottled by the
proprietors as a single grain,
but now several expressions of
Girvan Patent Still are available.
Older expressions are generally
dominated by the maize component
and are greatly softened by age
to provide a delicate and refined
whisky of some subtlety and
delightful complexity.

GIRVAN PATENT STILL
NO. 4 APPS ▶

SINGLE GRAIN 42% ABV
The nose yields citrus fruit and brittle
toffee, while the palate is glossy, with
spicy fruit. Faint spice and watery
toffee in the finish.

WHISKEYS

G

GREAT

GLEN BRETON

Canada

Glenora Distillery, Route 19, Glenville,
Cape Breton, Nova Scotia
www.glenoradistillery.com

This is North America's only
malt whisky distillery. Cape
Breton Island has a strong Scottish
heritage, but the Scotch Whisky
Association has criticized the
name for sounding too much
like a Scotch.

Production began in June 1990,
halting within weeks due to lack
of funds. The distillery was later
bought by Lauchie MacLean,
who has re-distilled earlier,
inconsistent spirit, and bottles
at 8 or 9 years.

Glenora has its own maltings
and uses Scottish barley that is
given a light peating. The two
stills it uses are made by Forsyths
of Rothes.

◀ GLEN BRETON RARE

SINGLE MALT 43% ABV
A butterscotch, heather, ground
ginger, and honey nose. Light to
medium body, with a creamy
mouthfeel and notes of wood,
almonds, caramel, and peat.

GLEN DEVERON

Scotland
Macduff Distillery, Banff, Aberdeenshire

While the single malt is Glen Deveron (named after the water source—the Deveron River in eastern Speyside), the distillery is called Macduff. It was founded in 1962 by a consortium led by the Duff family. Much of the malt was used in blends, particularly William Lawson, whose owners bought the distillery in 1972. Since then it has changed hands twice, increased its number of stills to five, and now belongs to Bacardi. Various age statements are produced, and, just to confuse matters, there are occasional independent bottlings under the name Macduff.

GLEN DEVERON 10-YEAR-OLD ▶

SINGLE MALT: HIGHLANDS 40% ABV
Although it is described as a "Pure Highland Single Malt" on the bottle's label, in style this is a classic, clean, gentle Speyside whisky.

GLEN ELGIN

Scotland
Longmorn, Morayshire
www.malts.com

The Glen Elgin distillery was founded in 1898, when demand for Speyside malt from the blenders was at its peak.

But boom soon turned to bust, the industry entered a long slump, and production at Glen Elgin was intermittent during its first three decades, as the business passed from one owner to the next.

After many years of appearing only in blends (notably White Horse), a first distillery bottling of Glen Elgin was released in 1977.

◄ GLEN ELGIN 12-YEAR-OLD
SINGLE MALT: SPEYSIDE 43% ABV
This is one of the most floral and perfumed Speyside malts, with a nutty, honey-blossom aroma and a balanced flavor that goes from sweet to dry.

GLEN ELGIN 16-YEAR-OLD
SINGLE MALT: SPEYSIDE 58.5% ABV
The 16-year-old is a non–chill filtered, cask-strength malt with a deep mahogany color and a ripe, fruitcake flavor from its years in European oak.

GLEN GARIOCH

Scotland

Oldmeldrum, Inverurie,
Aberdeenshire
www.glengarioch.com

This small Aberdeenshire distillery
was founded in 1798, yet the first
distillery bottling of Glen Garioch
as a single malt was not until
1972. It survived the long years
in between thanks to its
popularity among blenders.

Glen Garioch is now part of
Morrison Bowmore, which bottles
most of the distillery's limited
production as a single malt.

GLEN GARIOCH VIRGIN OAK ▶

SINGLE MALT: HIGHLANDS 48% ABV
Ripe peaches on the nose, spicy oak,
vanilla, and developing floral notes.
The palate yields malt, milk chocolate,
nougat, orange, and a hint of cloves.

GLEN GARIOCH
FOUNDER'S RESERVE

SINGLE MALT: HIGHLANDS 48% ABV
Pears, peaches, and apricots on the
nose, plus butterscotch and vanilla.
Relatively full-bodied, with a palate of
vanilla, malt, melon, and subtle smoke.

GLEN GRANT

Scotland

Rothes, Morayshire
www.glengrant.com

Glen Grant, built in 1840, was the first of the five distilleries in the town of Rothes. It was a very good site for a distillery, with the Glen Grant burn supplying water for the mash and to power the machinery, and plentiful supplies of grain from the barley fields of nearby Moray.

Having passed through the hands of Pernod Ricard in 2001–2006, it is now with the Italian Campari drinks group. Though it receives little attention at home, it is one of the top five best-selling malts in the world.

◄ GLEN GRANT 10-YEAR-OLD

SINGLE MALT: SPEYSIDE 40% ABV
A relatively dry nose with the scent of orchard fruit. Light to medium body with a cereal, nutty flavor.

GLEN GRANT 18-YEAR-OLD

SINGLE MALT: SPEYSIDE 43% ABV
The nose is fresh and fruity, with more depth and fragrance than younger expressions. Rich on the fruity palate, with milk chocolate, sweet spices, brittle toffee, and a hint of creamy oak.

GLEN KEITH

Scotland
Keith, Banffshire

Having bought Strathisla in 1950, Seagram built Glen Keith on the site of an old corn mill seven years later. Both are in Keith and were part of Seagram's whisky arm, Chivas Brothers (now part of Pernod Ricard). Both also shared a simple function—to supply the company's best-selling blended brands. Glen Keith began life using triple distillation and later pioneered the use of computers in its whisky-making at a time when some distilleries had only recently joined the national grid.

Glen Keith was mothballed in 2000 but re-opened in 2013 after major refurbishment.

**GLEN KEITH 19-YEAR-OLD
CASK STRENGTH** ▶

SINGLE MALT: SPEYSIDE 56.3% ABV
Banoffee pie, ginger, and raisins on the nose. The viscous palate yields sherry, fudge, and white pepper.

GLEN ORD

Scotland
Muir of Ord, Ross-shire

Despite its name, Glen Ord is not in a valley, but on the fertile flatlands of the Black Isle, north of Inverness. It was founded in 1838, close to the alleged site of the Ferintosh Distillery, which was established in the 1670s. In 1923 Glen Ord was bought by John Dewar & Sons, shortly before they joined the Distiller's Company Limited (DCL).

With 14 stills and a 2.4-million-gallon (11-million-liter) production, it has plenty to spare for a single malt. Confusingly, this has been called Ord, Glenordie, and Muir of Ord at various times. Recent bottlings are called The Singleton of Glen Ord, aiming at the Asian market.

◀ THE SINGLETON OF GLEN ORD 12-YEAR-OLD

SINGLE MALT: HIGHLANDS 40% ABV
The nose is nutty, with honey, milk chocolate, and Turkish delight. Relatively light-bodied, with cinnamon, sherry, toffee, apples, and a hint of milky coffee.

GLEN SCOTIA

Scotland
Campbeltown, Argyll
www.glenscotia.com

Strung out at the far end of the
Mull of Kintyre, Campbeltown's
rise and fall as "whiskyopolis" has
been well documented, as has the
story of the Springbank Distillery's
survival and subsequent cult
status (*see p319*). Meanwhile, the
much lesser known Glen Scotia
also survived. With its single pair
of stills, Campbeltown's "other"
distillery was founded in the
1830s by the Galbraith family,
who retained control for the rest
of the century. After various
owners followed, it was bought
by Loch Lomond Group, part of
Exponent Private Equity, in 2014.

GLEN SCOTIA DOUBLE CASK ▶
SINGLE MALT: CAMPBELTOWN
46% ABV
Sweet on the nose, with brambles,
red currants, vanilla, and toffee. More
vanilla on the smooth palate, with
ginger, spicy sherry, and finally a
suggestion of sea salt.

GLEN SPEY

Scotland
Rothes, Aberlour, Banffshire
www.malts.com

James Stuart was an established distiller with Macallan and the key partner in building the Glenrothes Distillery in 1878, although he quickly pulled out of that venture. A few years later, he decided to convert an oat mill he owned into Glen Spey, on the opposite bank of the Rothes Burn from Glenrothes. The project inevitably led to disputes over water rights. In 1887, Glen Spey was sold to the London-based gin distiller Gilbey's, who later merged with Justerini & Brooks. Its J&B blend has contained Glen Spey ever since. The current owners, Diageo, have just one malt bottling in their Flora & Fauna range.

◀ **GLEN SPEY FLORA & FAUNA 12-YEAR-OLD**
SINGLE MALT: SPEYSIDE 43% ABV
A light, grassy nose and brisk, nutty flavor. Very dry, with a short finish.

GLENALLACHIE

Scotland
Aberlour, Banffshire

This modern gravity-flow distillery
was established by a subsidiary
of the giant Scottish & Newcastle
Breweries in 1967. The architect
was William Delmé-Evans, who
had earlier designed and part-
owned Tullibardine and Jura. With
the capacity to produce 615,000
gallons (2.8 million liters) of pure
alcohol a year, there should be
plenty available for a single malt.
And yet, so far there have only
been a few independent bottlings
and a 16-year-old cask strength
expression. In July 2017, Pernod
Ricard sold Glenallachie to a
consortium led by whisky
entrepreneur Billy Walker.

**GLENALLACHIE
16-YEAR-OLD 1990 ▶**

SINGLE MALT: SPEYSIDE 56.9% ABV
A dark, heavily sherried whisky
matured in first-fill Oloroso casks,
which can be hard to find.

GLENBURGIE

Scotland
Glenburgie, Forres, Morayshire

Glenburgie began life as the Kilnflat Distillery in 1829. It was renamed Glenburgie in 1878 and, after various changes in ownership, became part of Canada's Hiram Walker in the 1930s. From then on, the primary role of this distillery was to supply whisky for Ballantine's Finest. Yet, as early as 1958, long before most of Speyside began thinking of single malt, Glenburgie released its own bottling under the name Glencraig. In 2004, its then owners, Allied Distillers, demonstrated their faith in Glenburgie by investing $7.9 million. The distillery was completely rebuilt and only the stills and milling equipment were kept.

◀ **GLENBURGIE 10-YEAR-OLD**
SINGLE MALT: SPEYSIDE 40% ABV
The nose offers fudge, vanilla, honey, malt, and soft oak. Creamy mouthfeel.

GLENCADAM

Scotland

Brechin, Angus
www.glencadamdistillery.co.uk

With the demise of Lochside in 2005, Glencadam became the only distillery left in Angus. It was founded in 1825 by George Cooper and, despite various changes in ownership, remained in private hands until 1954, when it became part of Hiram Walker and later Allied Distillers. While there was some safety in numbers on Speyside, Glencadam looked increasingly isolated. When it shut down in 2000—a victim of overproduction in the industry—its prospects looked bleak. But it slipped back into independent hands in 2003 when bought by Angus Dundee (*see p17*).

GLENCADAM 10-YEAR-OLD ▶
SINGLE MALT: HIGHLANDS 46% ABV
The nose is fresh and grassy, with citrus notes and a trace of spicy oak. Rounded on the palate, citrusy and crisp. Well-balanced, with a long finish.

G

GLENDALOUGH

Ireland

*Glendalough Distillery,
Glendalough, County Wicklow
www.glendaloughdistillery.com*

Glendalough distillery was established in 2013, purchasing a still made in Germany's Black Forest region. The company had actually already been trading for two years at that point, offering a range of poteen and whiskeys sourced from other distillers.

Glendalough currently markets 7- and 13-year-old single malts, and an innovative single grain whiskey, matured initially for three years and six months in ex-bourbon barrels, and then finished for six months in Spanish Oloroso sherry casks.

◄ GLENDALOUGH SINGLE GRAIN DOUBLE BARREL

SINGLE GRAIN 42% ABV

Light on the nose, with Christmas pudding aromas. The palate features honey, vanilla, dried fruit, and a hint of pepper. Ginger and almonds in the finish.

GLENDRONACH

Scotland
Forgue, Huntly, Aberdeenshire

This distillery is the spiritual sister to Ardmore, and fellow contributor to the Teacher's blend. Although William Teacher & Sons did not buy Glendronach until 1960, the firm had sourced Glendronach malts for years. After Teacher's was swallowed up by Allied Distillers, Glendronach was picked, in 1991, to be one of the "Caledonian Malts"— the company's belated riposte to UDV's Classic Malts. A decade later, after five years in mothballs, the distillery re-opened. By that time the single malts had become less peaty and were matured in American oak ex-bourbon casks rather than sherry casks.

GLENDRONACH 12-YEAR-OLD ▶

SINGLE MALT: SPEYSIDE 40% ABV
This dense, heavily sherried malt replaced the 15-year-old and is best suited to after-dinner sipping.

GLENDULLAN

Scotland
Dufftown, Keith, Banffshire
www.malts.com

There were already six distilleries in Dufftown when the Aberdeen-based blenders William Williams & Sons decided to build a seventh. Work on Glendullan began in 1897, and within five years its whisky had secured a royal warrant from the new king, Edward VII. The distillery has been in almost continual production ever since. In the 1960s, a modern distillery was erected next door. Although both facilities continued in tandem for 20 years, now the modern distillery carries on alone. Since 2007, Singleton of Glendullan bottlings have been available in the US.

◄ **GLENDULLAN FLORA & FAUNA 12-YEAR-OLD**
SINGLE MALT: SPEYSIDE 43% ABV
A crisp, apéritif-style malt with a sweeter palate than you would expect.

GLENFARCLAS

Scotland
Ballindalloch, Banffshire
www.glenfarclas.co.uk

The oldest family-owned distillery
in Scotland has belonged to the
Grants since 1865, when John
Grant and his son George took over
the tenancy of Rechlarich farm,
near Ballindalloch. It gradually
assumed importance in the family
business, and went on to become
the Glenfarclas-Glenlivet Distillery
Company in partnership with the
Pattison Brothers of Leith, whose
bankruptcy at the end of the
19th century almost dragged
the Glenfarclas distillery down
with it. ☞

GLENFARCLAS 105 ▶
SINGLE MALT: SPEYSIDE 60% ABV
A cask strength 10-year-old. Water
dampens the fiery edge and brings
out a sweet, nutty-spicy character.

GLENFARCLAS 10-YEAR-OLD
SINGLE MALT: SPEYSIDE 40% ABV
This rich, malty whisky with
a smoky, aromatic nose is a nod
to the Highlands.

GLENFARCLAS

Surrounded by 10 large dunnage warehouses, Glenfarclas is no boutique distillery. It boasts a modern mill and six stills. It also claims to be the first malt distillery to have offered a cask strength expression—Glenfarclas 105 was released in 1968. At the time, the industry doubted that single malts, let alone something that was 60 percent pure alcohol, would catch on with the whiskey buyer.

Recently, Glenfarclas offered 10 vintage expressions, ranging from 1952 to 1989. The house style is a robust, outdoors take on Speyside, with a greater affiliation to sherry butts than bourbon barrels.

◀ **GLENFARCLAS 12-YEAR-OLD**
SINGLE MALT: SPEYSIDE 43% ABV
A distinct sherry nose, with spicy flavors of cinnamon and stewed fruit.

GLENFARCLAS 15-YEAR-OLD
SINGLE MALT: SPEYSIDE 46% ABV
Described by writer Dave Broom as "George Melly in a glass," for its fruity, over-the-top exuberance. It is intensely perfumed, sherried, and powerful.

GLENFIDDICH

Scotland

Dufftown, Keith, Banffshire
www.glenfiddich.com

With a wife and nine children to support on a salary of $486 a year, William Grant had to scrimp and save until he raised the funds to start Glenfiddich in 1886. Using stones from the bed of the River Fiddich, and secondhand stills from neighboring Cardhu, he was able to produce his first spirit on Christmas Day 1887. From these humble beginnings, Glenfiddich has grown into the biggest malt distillery in the world. By the time William Grant died in 1923, his ☛

GLENFIDDICH 12-YEAR-OLD ▶
SINGLE MALT: SPEYSIDE 40% ABV
A gentle, apéritif-style whisky with a malty, grassy flavor and a little vanilla sweetness. Quite soft.

GLENFIDDICH 15-YEAR-OLD SOLERA RESERVE
SINGLE MALT: SPEYSIDE 40% ABV
After 15 years in American oak, this is finished off in Spanish casks for an extra-soft layer of fresh fruit and spice.

GLENFIDDICH

firm was already producing its own blends, which were sold as far afield as Australia and Canada. The company also pioneered today's market for single malts in the 1960s—there was no big brand before Glenfiddich.

Today Glenfiddich has 31 stills and a capacity of 3.1 million gallons (14 million liters) of pure alcohol a year. This makes it the most productive malt distillery in Scotland, with significantly greater capacity than Diageo's Roseisle Distillery. Having been the world's best-selling single malt since 1963, Glenfiddich was finally overtaken by The Glenlivet in 2014.

◀ GLENFIDDICH 18-YEAR-OLD SOLERA RESERVE

SINGLE MALT: SPEYSIDE 40% ABV
A big step up from the 12-year-old: ripe tropical fruit flavors, a pleasant oaky sweetness, and a trace of sherry.

GLENFIDDICH 21-YEAR-OLD CARIBBEAN RUM CASK

SINGLE MALT: SPEYSIDE 40% ABV
Rich, toffee-flavored malt with flavors of bananas, caramel, spice, and chocolate orange.

GLENGLASSAUGH

Scotland
Portsoy, Banffshire
www.glenglassaugh.com

Glenglassaugh was founded by Aberdeenshire entrepreneur James Moir in the 1870s at a cost of $55,000. Although it was also renovated and expanded, it was sold for only $73,000 20 years later, when it was bought by blender Robertson & Baxter, now called Edrington. The distillery has had periodic bursts of production, but has spent much of its life in mothballs. When its stills went cold before the millennium, many feared that Glenglassaugh was doomed. It was rescued by a private consortium, however, and was reopened in 2008. Glenglassaugh is now owned by Brown-Forman.

GLENGLASSAUGH EVOLUTION ▶

SINGLE MALT: HIGHLANDS
50% ABV

The nose offers toffee, ginger, peaches, and vanilla. Orchard fruits, caramel, and coconut on the palate.

Whiskey Tour:
SPEYSIDE

Speyside boasts the greatest concentration of distilleries in the world. Distillery tours were pioneered here, when William Grant & Sons first opened Glenfiddich to the public in 1969. Its competitors laughed—but soon opened their own centers. Speyside hosts two whisky festivals each year, in May and September. Convenient accommodation options include the Highlander Inn in Craigellachie and The Mash Tun in Aberlour.

SCOTLAND

DAY 1: GLENFIDDICH, THE BALVENIE

❶ Begin at Dufftown's **Glenfiddich**, the ultimate home of whisky tourism. The distillery offers a free tour or an extended option with tastings at extra cost. You need to pre-book for the extended tour, which lasts two and a half hours.

❷ After lunch at Glenfiddich, take in sister distillery **The Balvenie**. The three-hour guided tour here, which must also be pre-booked, includes the floor maltings and tastings of exclusive vintages.

THE BALVENIE

DAY 2: COOPERAGE, ABERLOUR, THE MACALLAN, CARDHU

❸ Head to Craigellachie to start the day at the **Speyside Cooperage**. There you can watch a film about cask-making and see the coopers at work from a viewing gallery.

ABERLOUR CASKS

❹ Afterward, take the A95 toward **Aberlour** Distillery, which is the next stop. Again, pre-booking is advisable. The tour culminates in a tasting and the chance to bottle your own whisky from the cask.

FORRES

A96

NAIRN

A939

MILL BU

A939

B9007

CÀRN
NA LÒIN

GRANTOWN-
ON-SPEY ❼

A95

A9

A95

Spey

NETHY BRIDGE

BOAT OF GARTEN

AVIEMORE

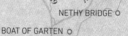

miles
0   5
0   5
kilometers

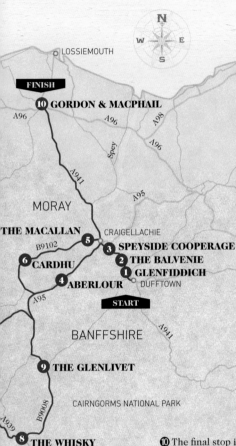

LOSSIEMOUTH

N W E S

FINISH

❿ GORDON & MACPHAIL

A96

A96

A98

A96

Spey

A941

A95

MORAY

THE MACALLAN

CRAIGELLACHIE

B9102

❺

❸ SPEYSIDE COOPERAGE

❻ CARDHU

❷ THE BALVENIE

❹ ABERLOUR

❶ GLENFIDDICH

DUFFTOWN

A95

START

BANFFSHIRE

A941

❾ THE GLENLIVET

B9008

CAIRNGORMS NATIONAL PARK

A939

❽ THE WHISKY CASTLE

TOUR STATISTICS

DAYS: 3
LENGTH: 90 miles (145km)
TRAVEL: Car, or bus and taxi
DISTILLERIES: 8

❺ Head over the Spey, pausing to admire the Thomas Telford bridge (built in 1812), then take the B9102 to **The Macallan**. Its "Precious Tour" is the one to pre-book for its tutored nosing and tasting of a range of Macallan whiskies.

❻ **Cardhu** Distillery is farther along the B9102, and you can visit without pre-booking. The malt made here is used in the Johnnie Walker blends.

DAY 3: GRANTOWN-ON-SPEY, THE WHISKY CASTLE, THE GLENLIVET, GORDON & MACPHAIL

❼ **Grantown-on-Spey** is the gateway to the Cairngorms National Park. It's a handy place to pick up provisions, and has a good little whisky shop on the High Street called the Wee Spey Dram.

❽ Head east from Grantown to get to Tomintoul, where **The Whisky Castle** shop has an excellent selection of Scotch malts.

❾ Pre-register on **The Glenlivet** website (*www.theglenlivet.com*) as a "Guardian" to gain access to a secret room where you can enjoy some unusual drams. The free tour is a good introduction to the oldest legal distillery on Speyside; better still is its three-day Whisky School.

❿ The final stop is a place of pilgrimage for serious whisky fans: the **Gordon & MacPhail** shop in Elgin. Here you'll find all your favorites, some rare bottles, and exceptional value in G&M's own bottlings from their vast stock of whiskies.

GORDON & MACPHAIL

GLENGOYNE

Scotland
Drumgoyne, Stirlingshire
www.glengoyne.com

The Campsie Fells were once
a hotbed of whisky smuggling.
Before the Excise Act of 1823,
there were at least 18 illicit
distillers in this corner of
Stirlingshire. Among them was
probably George Connell, who
finally took out a license for his
Burnfoot Distillery in 1833. It
went on to become Glenguin and
eventually Glengoyne in 1905.

◀ GLENGOYNE 10-YEAR-OLD
SINGLE MALT: HIGHLANDS 40% ABV
This unpeated whisky has a clean,
grassy aroma, with a nutty sweetness
that comes through on the palate.

GLENGOYNE 12-YEAR-OLD CASK STRENGTH
SINGLE MALT: HIGHLANDS
57.2% ABV
Non–chill filtered and bottled at cask
strength, it has a light sweet nose, with
notes of heather, pear drops, and
marzipan. Malty, cereal palate,
seasoned with black pepper.

By then the distillery was owned by the blending house of Lang Brothers, who were bought out in the 1960s by Robertson & Baxter, now Edrington.

In 2001 it released a novel expression of Glengoyne, involving the first ever use of Scottish oak casks. Two years later, the distillery was sold to the blender and bottler Ian MacLeod & Co. The number of single malts has grown dramatically and includes single-cask bottlings alongside the core range.

GLENGOYNE 21-YEAR-OLD ▶

SINGLE MALT: HIGHLANDS 43% ABV
This is a rich, after-dinner malt, with notes of brandy butter, cinnamon, and sweet spice.

GLENGOYNE 18-YEAR-OLD

SINGLE MALT: HIGHLANDS 43% ABV
Milk chocolate, vanilla, melon, and grapefruit on the nose. The palate is rich, with cinnamon and ginger, almonds, and orange marmalade.

GLENKINCHIE

Scotland

Pencaitland, Tranent, East Lothian
www.malts.com

Robert Burns described the rolling farmland south of Edinburgh as "the most glorious corn country I have ever seen," and it was here at Pencaitland that John and George Rate founded Glenkinchie in 1825.

In more recent history, the Glenkinchie 10-year-old was picked as one of the original Classic Malts by Diageo in 1988. New expressions have recently been added, and the 10 has been replaced with a 12-year-old.

◀ GLENKINCHIE 12-YEAR-OLD

SINGLE MALT: LOWLANDS 43% ABV
The nose reveals a sweet, grassy aroma with a faint wisp of smoke. In the mouth it has a firm, cereal flavor and a touch of spice at the end.

GLENKINCHIE 20-YEAR-OLD

SINGLE MALT: LOWLANDS
58.4% ABV
Aged in bourbon casks and then reracked into brandy barrels, the 20-year-old has a luscious, mouth-coating texture and plenty of spicy, stewed fruit flavors.

THE GLENLIVET

Scotland

Ballindalloch, Banffshire
www.theglenlivet.com

In the early 19th century, Glen
Livet was a glen dedicated to
making moonshine after the
harvest—there were at least 200
illicit stills in this small corner of
Speyside. Among them was George
Smith, who in 1824 established
Glenlivet as a licensed distillery.
But breaking ranks with the
smuggling fraternity meant that
Smith had to carry revolvers for
his protection.

Smith began supplying Andrew
Usher in Edinburgh who

THE GLENLIVET
12-YEAR-OLD ▶

SINGLE MALT: SPEYSIDE 40% ABV
Citrusy and heathery, with a scent
of fresh wood and soft fruit, a light to
medium body, and a dry, clean finish.

THE GLENLIVET FRENCH OAK
RESERVE 15-YEAR-OLD

SINGLE MALT: SPEYSIDE 40% ABV
A smoother, richer take on the
12-year-old, with a malty, strawberries-
and-cream flavor laced with spice.

THE GLENLIVET

 bottled a prototype blend, Old Vatted Glenlivet, in 1853. As blended Scotch took off, demand for "Glenlivet-style" malts to feed the blends soared.

Glenlivet was bought by Pernod Ricard in 2001, who expanded its core range. During 2009 and 2010, the capacity of Glenlivet was dramatically increased to 2.3 million gallons (10.5 million liters) per annum as Pernod's whisky division, Chivas Brothers, sought to overtake Glenfiddich as the world's best-selling single malt. That ambition was finally achieved in 2014.

◄ THE GLENLIVET XXV

SINGLE MALT: SPEYSIDE 43% ABV
This 25-year-old is a sumptuous after-dinner malt of real complexity, with flavors of candied orange peel and raisins and an intense nutty, spicy character.

THE GLENLIVET 18-YEAR-OLD

SINGLE MALT: SPEYSIDE 43% ABV
This whisky has far more depth and character than the standard 12-year-old. Honeyed, fragrant, and dries to a long, nutty finish.

GLENLOSSIE

Scotland
Elgin, Morayshire
www.malts.com

Glenlossie was built in 1876 by
John Duff, the former manager of
Glendronach. For a century it was
a single entity, and part of DCL
from 1919. Its role was simply to
pump out malt whisky for blends.
Yet, within the industry, the
quality of Glenlossie was
appreciated and it was one of
only a dozen to be designated
"top class." It now shares its site
with Mannochmore, a new
distillery built in 1971.

Glenlossie has produced a
10-year-old since 1990, although
there have been a fair number
of independent bottlings from
Gordon & MacPhail, among others.

GLENLOSSIE FLORA & FAUNA
10-YEAR-OLD ▶

SINGLE MALT: SPEYSIDE 43% ABV
Grassy and heathery, with a smooth,
mouth-coating texture and a long
spicy finish.

GLENMORANGIE

Scotland

Tain, Ross-shire
www.glenmorangie.com

Glenmorangie started life as an old farm distillery, but was licensed in 1843 by William Matheson, who was already involved with Balblair. It remained a rustic operation for years. In the 1880s Alfred Barnard described Glenmorangie as "the most ancient and primitive we have seen" and "almost in ruins."

Outside investors were brought in just in time and the distillery was rebuilt. For much of the 20th century, its key role was to supply malt for blends such as Highland

◀ GLENMORANGIE ORIGINAL

SINGLE MALT: HIGHLANDS 40% ABV
This is the ever-popular 10-year-old. It has honeyed flavors with a hint of almonds.

GLENMORANGIE 18-YEAR-OLD

SINGLE MALT: HIGHLANDS 43% ABV
A rich, well-rounded whisky, with dried fruit notes and a distinctive nuttiness from its finishing in sherry butts.

Queen and James Martin's. In the 1970s, though, Glenmorangie started laying down casks for a 10-year-old single malt. It was the best decision the company ever made—by the late 1990s, this had become the best-selling single malt in Scotland.

Glenmorangie's stills are tall and thin, and produce a light, very pure spirit. The real skill of the distillery has been in the way it has combined this elegant spirit with wood—indeed, Glenmorangie has been a pioneer of wood finishes. After endless experiments with increasingly exotic barrels, it has become an expert in how particular casks can twist and refocus a mature malt before bottling.

GLENMORANGIE 25-YEAR-OLD ▶
SINGLE MALT: HIGHLANDS 43% ABV
Packed with flavor, this produces dried fruit, berries, chocolate, and spice. An intense and complex whisky.

GLENMORANGIE NECTAR D'OR
SINGLE MALT: HIGHLANDS 46% ABV
Here, the Glenmorangie honeyed floral character is given a twist of spice and lemon tart from Sauternes casks.

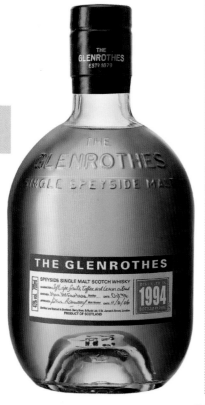

GLENROTHES

Scotland
Rothes, Morayshire
www.glenrotheswhisky.com

After Dufftown, Rothes is the
second busiest whisky town on
Speyside. Not that you would
know it: the distilleries are tucked
discreetly out of sight, including
Glenrothes, which sits quietly in
a dip beside the Rothes burn.

After its founding in 1878,
Glenrothes began to build a
reputation among blenders for the
quality of its malt. It seemed as if
there was never any to spare—
until 1987, when the first single

◀ THE GLENROTHES 1994
SINGLE MALT: SPEYSIDE 43% ABV
A satisfyingly complex malt with
a fruity, toffee-scented bouquet that
leads to a soft citrus flavor and long,
gentle finish.

THE GLENROTHES 1978
SINGLE MALT: SPEYSIDE 43% ABV
A very rare expression, released in
2008, with a concentrated plum
pudding and molasses character, a
silky, honeyed texture and great length.

malt, a 12-year-old was released. At first, Glenrothes failed to stand out: it had entered the 12-year-old stakes late in the day and there was plenty of competition, particularly on Speyside.

This all changed with the launch of the highly acclaimed Glenrothes Vintage malt in 1994. The brand owners, wine merchants Berry Brothers & Rudd, realized vintage variation might be appreciated by malt-whisky-lovers as well as wine-lovers. In 2004, Glenrothes Select Reserve was released to provide continuity between vintages.

THE GLENROTHES SELECT RESERVE ▶

SINGLE MALT: SPEYSIDE 43% ABV
Like non-vintage Champagne, this is a vatting of different ages to produce a complex whisky with notes of hard candy, ripe fruit, vanilla, and spice. Sweeter on the nose than in the mouth.

THE GLENROTHES 1975 ▶

SINGLE MALT: SPEYSIDE 43% ABV
Increasingly hard to find, this vintage offers big, rich flavors—stewed fruits, toffee, bitter chocolate, and orange peel. Medium-sweet satisfying finish.

GLENTAUCHERS

Scotland
Mulben, Keith, Banffshire

Many late-Victorian distilleries sprang up in the hope of finding a market among whisky blenders but, in 1897, Glentauchers was built explicitly to supply Buchanan's blend, which evolved into the top-selling Black & White. The distillery was a joint venture between James Buchanan and the Glasgow-based blender W. P. Lowrie. They chose an ideal site, right by a main road that connected to the east-coast train line from Aberdeen to Inverness. Now owned by Pernod Ricard, Glentauchers has the same principal role it always had—supplying malt for blends.

◀ GLENTAUCHERS GORDON & MACPHAIL 1991

SINGLE MALT: SPEYSIDE 43% ABV
This 16-year-old Gordon & MacPhail bottling has a sweet, sherried character, with a subtle smoky flavor.

THE GLENTURRET

Scotland
Crieff, Perthshire
www.theglenturret.com

This small Perthshire distillery, first licensed in 1775, claims to be the oldest working distillery in Scotland.

Today Glenturret is known as the spiritual home of The Famous Grouse *(see p117)*, an association showcased at its visitor center and its Famous Grouse Whisky School, which offers a one-day malt whisky course, including an in-depth distillery tour. Glenturret's other claim to fame is Towser, the cat, who won a place in *The Guinness Book of Records* for killing nearly 30,000 mice.

GLENTURRET 10-YEAR-OLD ▶
SINGLE MALT: HIGHLANDS 40% ABV
Replacing the 12-year-old, this floral, vanilla-scented malt is now the main Glenturret expression.

THE GLENTURRET PEATED
SINGLE MALT: HIGHLANDS 59.7% ABV
Furniture polish, pineapple, and rosehip on the nose. Fruity palate of chocolate, vanilla, and allspice.

GOLD COCK

Czech Republic

Jelínek Distillery,
Razov 472, 76312 Vizovice
www.rjelinek.cz

Jelínek Distillery was founded at the end of the 19th century, and acquired the Gold Cock brand from Tešetice, a Czech distillery that no longer exists. For its two expressions—Red Feathers and a 12-year-old—Jelínek uses Moravian barley and water is sourced from an underground well that is rich in minerals. The type of cask used is not specified.

◄ **GOLD COCK RED FEATHERS**
BLEND 40% ABV
Light and grainy, slightly metallic, and sweetish.

GOLDLYS

Belgium
Graanstokerij Filliers,
Leernsesteenweg 5, 9800 Deinze
www.filliers.be

The Flemish distiller Filliers has been making grain spirits since 1880. In 2008 it surprised the whiskey world by launching two whiskies it had been maturing for years. Their name comes from the Lys River, which is nicknamed the "Golden River" because of the flax retted (soaked) in it. Goldlys uses malt, rye, and corn, and is distilled twice, first in a column still, then in a pot still—a similar process to making bourbon. The spirit is then matured in ex-bourbon casks, and a number of "finishes" are available.

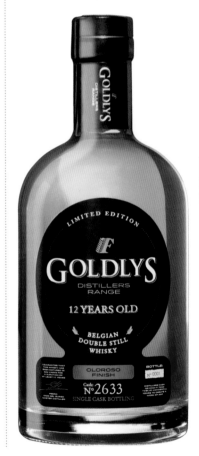

GOLDLYS 12-YEAR-OLD OLOROSO CASK FINISH ▶
DOUBLE STILL WHISKY 43% ABV
Vanilla, honey, and citrus on the nose. Oily palate of sherry and raisin leads to a lengthy finish.

GRAND MACNISH

Scotland
Owner: Macduff International

The long history of this brand dates back to Glasgow and 1863, when the original Robert McNish (an "a" crept into the brand name later), a grocer and general merchant, took up blending.

Grand Macnish Original still uses up to 40 whiskies in the blend, as was Robert McNish's practice. The distinctive bottle's label is graced by the McNish clan motto, *"Forti nihil difficile"* ("To the strong, nothing is difficult").

◀ GRAND MACNISH ORIGINAL
BLEND 40% ABV

Old leather and ripe fruits on the nose, giving way to a brandylike aroma. Noticeably sweet on the palate, with strong vanilla (wood) influences. A sustained and evolving finish, with some gentle smoke.

GRAND MACNISH 12-YEAR-OLD
BLEND 40% ABV

The extra age shows here in a fuller, rounder flavor with greater intensity and a more sustained finish.

GRANT'S

Scotland
Owner: William Grant & Sons
www.grantswhisky.com

This staunchly independent
company has prospered on
Speyside since 1887 and
remains in private hands. Today
it is famous for Glenfiddich and
its sister single malt, Balvenie,
but it also produces a third malt,
Kininvie, which is reserved for
blending. In addition, it has a
grain distillery at Girvan and
a single malt distillery at Ailsa
Bay, which opened in 2008. ☛

GRANT'S SIGNATURE ▶
BLEND 40% ABV
Soft citrus fruits, barley, vanilla, and
almonds on the nose. Nutty spices,
milky coffee, and caramel shortcake
on the palate. Coffee turns to cocoa
powder in the finish, accompanied
by light oak notes.

GRANT'S 25-YEAR-OLD
BLEND 40% ABV
Mellow on the nose; warm, floral,
and peachy, with butter, vanilla, worn
leather, and a whiff of smoke. Fresh
fruits, spice, discreet vanilla, ginger,
and oak on the palate.

GRANT'S

The first Ailsa Bay single malt was released in 2016, and it is a heavily peated whisky, comprising spirit matured in four different types of cask.

The company is determined to maintain close control over their supplies of whisky, and with good reason: Grant's Family Reserve blend broke through the 1 million case barrier as long ago as 1979. The blended range of whiskies continues to evolve, while still remaining true to the mark of quality associated with its distinctive triangular bottle.

◀ GRANT'S ALE CASK RESERVE
BLEND 40% ABV

Grant's has ventured into special wood finishes with great success. This is the only Scotch whisky to be finished in barrels that have previously held beer. Ale casks give the whisky a uniquely creamy, malty, and honeyed taste.

GRANT'S SHERRY CASK RESERVE
BLEND 40% ABV

Prepared in the same way as the groundbreaking ale cask version, but here the whisky is finished in Spanish Oloroso sherry casks, giving it a warm, rich, and fruity palate.

GREEN SPOT

Ireland
*Midleton Distillery, Midleton,
County Cork*

In the days before distillers in Ireland spent millions on building brands, they simply used to make the stuff, leaving the filthy job of selling the whiskey to bonders like Mitchell's. This, of course, was a terrible business plan: it allowed the Scots to build global brands, while the Irish were obsessed with an ever-shrinking domestic market. By the time the Irish got back into the race in the 1960s, Irish whiskey had a miserable 1 percent of the global whiskey market. Green Spot is the last bonder's own label. Owned by Mitchell's of Dublin, it's a pure pot still whiskey, made in Midleton.

GREEN SPOT ▶

PURE POT STILL 40% ABV

Green Spot is matured for just six to eight years, but a glass of this is still bracing stuff, with a wonderful, lightly sherried finish. One of a kind.

GUILLON

France
Hameau de Vertuelle, 51150 Louvois, Champagne
www.distillerie-guillon.com

The Guillon Distillery is located in the Champagne region of France, and was purpose-built in 1997 to produce whisky. It started distilling in 1999, distinguishing itself by the use of a variety of ex-wine casks for maturation. For the first maturation period, ex-Burgundy casks are used. After that, the whisky is finished for six months in casks that used to contain sweet wines like Banyuls, Loupiac, and Sauternes. Guillon bottles a premium blend at 40% ABV. The various single malts are bottled at 42, 43, and 46% ABV.

◄ GUILLON CUVÉE 42
SINGLE MALT 42% ABV
Barley, berry fruits, and a slight hint of smoke on the nose, with more barley plus apples, before a slightly ashy, fiery finish.

HAIG

Scotland
Owner: Diageo
www.haigwhisky.com

The distinguished name of Haig can trace its whisky-making pedigree back to the 17th century, when distilling began on the family farm. The company developed extensive interests in grain whisky distilling and was an early pioneer of blending. The company's Dimple brand (known as Pinch in the US, *see p103*) was a highly successful deluxe expression, and Haig was once the bestselling whisky in the UK. But its glory days are far behind it: today, under the control of Diageo, it is found mainly in Greece and the Canary Islands. During its heyday, the ubiquitous blend was advertised for many years with the strapline "Don't be vague—ask for Haig."

HAIG GOLD LABEL ▶
BLEND 40% ABV
Some sweetness on the nose, with faint smoky notes. Light and delicate, with soft wood notes and some spice on the finish, where a hint of smoke returns.

HAMMERHEAD

Czech Republic
www.stockspirits.com

Hammerhead whisky was distilled during 1989 at the Pradlo Distillery near Plzen, in western Czechoslovakia. The distillery had been making pot-still spirits for many years before experimenting with single malt whisky. This experiment is believed to be the only Bohemian single malt in the world.

Stock Spirits purchased the distillery without knowing of the whisky's existence. It was first bottled in 2011, and further releases have ensued since.

◀ HAMMERHEAD 25-YEAR-OLD

SINGLE MALT 40.7% ABV
A very drinkable whisky made from Czech barley and finished in casks made of Czech oak. It has a nutty, floral nose, spiced palate of dried fruit, and an oaky, licorice finish.

170

HANKEY BANNISTER

Scotland
Owner: Inver House Distillers

Founded by Messrs. Hankey and Bannister in 1757, the brand is now owned by Inver House Distillers, giving it access to a range of single malts from some of Scotland's most distinguished but lesser-known distilleries, such as Balblair, Balmenach, and Knockdhu. Key markets for Hankey Bannister include Latin America, Australia, and South America.

HANKEY BANNISTER 21-YEAR-OLD ▶
BLEND 43% ABV

A fresh and quite youthful nose. Soft and smooth, creamy toffee, with the vanilla house style coming through. Greater depth on the palate, with malty overtones and a warm finish.

HANKEY BANNISTER 40-YEAR-OLD
BLEND 43.3% ABV

Warm and fragrant aromas of raisin, chocolate, and citrus combine with spicy notes, leading to an exceptionally long lasting, smooth, full-bodied finish.

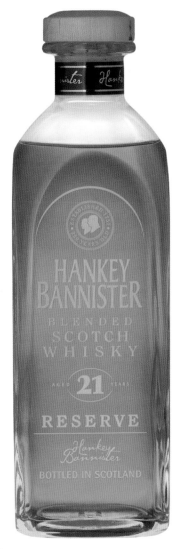

171

HANYU

Japan

Tao Shuzo, Saitama Prefecture
www.one-drinks.com

The Hanyu distillery was built by the Akuto family in the 1940s for producing shochu. Full production of whisky began in 1980, and Hanyu enjoyed success until the financial crisis of 1996 triggered the end of the whisky boom in Japan. The distillery had to close in 2000. When the firm was bought out in 2003, Ichiro Akuto was given a few months to buy back as much stock as he could before the distillery was demolished (*see Ichiro's Malt p185*).

◀ HANYU 1988 CASK 9501

SINGLE MALT 55.6% ABV
Vibrant and intense, with vanilla, some citrus, and a delicate cocoa-butter character. The Japanese oak adds a bittersweet edge. On the palate there's a rich depth. The finish shows smoke.

HAZELBURN

Scotland
Well Close, Campbeltown
www.springbankwhisky.com

Springbank Distillery is the great
survivor of the Campbeltown
whisky boom, which saw a
staggering 34 distilleries in town
in the 19th century. Today,
Springbank is a miniature malt-
whisky industry on its own, with
three separate distillations under
one roof: Springbank itself, the
pungently smoky Longrow, and
the light, gentle Hazelburn. As
well as using no peat in its malt,
Hazelburn—which was named
after an old, abandoned distillery
in Campbeltown—is triple-
distilled. The first spirit was
produced in 1997 and bottled
as an 8-year-old in 2005. The
oldest expression currently
available is a 12-year-old.

HAZELBURN 8-YEAR-OLD ▶
SINGLE MALT: CAMPBELTOWN
46% ABV
Lowland in style, clean and refreshing,
with a subtle, malty flavor.

173

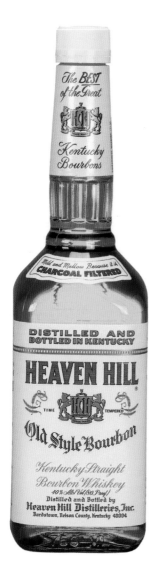

HEAVEN HILL

US

*1701 West Breckinridge Street,
Louisville, Kentucky*
www.heavenhill.com

Heaven Hill is the US's
largest independent producer
of distilled spirits to remain in
family ownership. When in 1996
the distillery and warehouses
were almost completely destroyed
by fire, the company purchased
Diageo's technologically advanced
Bernheim Distillery in Louisville,
and all production was moved
to that site.

Heaven Hill's specialty is older,
higher proof bourbons, traditional
in character, full-bodied, and
complex, such as Evan Williams
(*see p116*) and Elijah Craig (*see
p113*), but its diverse portfolio also
includes Bernheim Original (*see
p47*), Pikesville (*see p283*), and
Rittenhouse Rye (*see p296*).

◀ HEAVEN HILL
BOURBON 40% ABV

An excellent and competitively priced
"entry-level" bourbon, it has a nose
of oranges and cornbread, a sweet,
oily mouthfeel, and vanilla and corn
featuring on the well-balanced palate.

HELLYERS ROAD

Australia
153 Old Surrey Road,
Burnie, Tasmania
www.hellyersroaddistillery.com.au

Hellyers Road opened in 1999 and is owned by the Betta Milk Cooperative. It now has about 3,000 ex-bourbon casks under maturation, and also produces a Tasmanian barley-based, pot-still vodka. The experience gained in running a milk processing plant has provided owner Laurie House with all the knowledge he needs to run this modern and highly automated plant.

The distillery is named after Henry Hellyer who, in the 1820s, built the first road into the interior of Tasmania, the same road that now leads to the distillery.

HELLYERS ROAD ORIGINAL ▶
SINGLE MALT 46.2% ABV
A light-bodied, pale-colored malt, untinted and non–chill filtered. The nose is fresh and citric, with vanilla notes.

175

HIGH WEST

US

*27649 Old Lincoln Highway,
Wanship, Utah
www.highwest.com*

High West was established by
David Perkins during 2007 in
Park City, Utah. However, since
2015, distillation has taken place
in a 1,600-gallon (6,000-liter) pot
still at Blue Sky Ranch, Wanship, a
facility described by its owners as
"… the world's only distillery-
dude-ranch …!" High West makes
a variety of whiskeys, including
Valley Tan Utah oat whiskey and
the bourbon and rye "blend"
Bourye. The distillery is best
known for its ryes, especially
those released under the
Rendezvous label.

◀ HIGH WEST
RENDEZVOUS RYE

RYE WHISKEY 46% ABV
Rendezvous Rye is a blend of 16-
and 6-year-old rye. The nose offers
pepper and spice, vanilla, and toffee,
with an intense, sweet, fruity, smoky
palate and a long, spicy, caramel-
coated finish.

HIGHLAND PARK

Scotland
Kirkwall, Orkney
www.highlandpark.co.uk

Nowadays, Highland Park's far-flung Orkney island location is a great asset for the marketing of its whiskies but, for much of its history, the distance from its core market—the big blenders on the mainland— represented a major challenge for the island distillery. It survived, and now produces a Highland malt that is highly regarded. ☞

HIGHLAND PARK 12-YEAR-OLD ▶

SINGLE MALT: ISLANDS 40% ABV
This whisky has all-around quality. There are soft heather-honey flavors, some richer spicy notes, and an enveloping wisp of peat smoke that leaves the finish quite dry.

HIGHLAND PARK 18-YEAR-OLD

SINGLE MALT: ISLANDS 43% ABV
This is a touch sweeter than the 12-year-old, with notes of heather, toffee, and polished leather. The flavor of peat smoke comes through stronger on the finish than on the palate.

HIGHLAND PARK

🥄 Having invested in the brand, its owners have ambitious plans to reach the top ten.

Highland Park was first licensed to David Robertson in 1798 but since 1937 it has been part of Highland Distilleries (now the Edrington Group). To this day, a proportion of the barley is malted using the distillery's original floor maltings. The malt is then dried in a kiln, using local peat, which has a slightly sweeter aroma than that from Islay.

◀ HIGHLAND PARK 30-YEAR-OLD

SINGLE MALT: ISLANDS 48.1% ABV
The flagship of the range. Caramel sweetness, aromatic spices, dark chocolate, and orange notes. A long, drying, smoky finish, tinged with salt.

HIGHLAND PARK 25-YEAR-OLD

SINGLE MALT: ISLANDS 48.1% ABV
The deep amber color reveals plenty of contact with European oak. In fact, half of it was matured in first-fill sherry butts. Despite its age, it has a rich, nutty flavor, with dried fruits and scented smoke.

HIGHWOOD

Canada
*114 10th Avenue Southeast,
High River, Alberta
www.highwood-distillers.com*

Unusually for Canada, Highwood,
founded in 1974, is independently
owned. It makes a range of spirits
and is the only distillery in Canada
using just wheat in its column
stills as the base spirit for its
blends. In 2005, it bought the
Potter's and Cascadia distilleries.
Potter's is a separate brand from
Highwood. It is mixed with sherry,
which adds another dimension to
its flavor.

HIGHWOOD ▶
CANADIAN RYE 40% ABV
A blend of wheat and rye spirits. The
oaky, vanilla-scented nose has traces of
rye spice, orange blossom, and honey.
The palate balances sweetness with
oak tannins and nuts.

HIRSCH

Canada

*Distribution: Preiss Imports,
San Diego, California*

This whisky is no longer being
made, but is still available via a
US distributor. Although Canadian
whisky is often referred to as
"rye," only a few brands contain
more than 50 percent rye spirit,
which is what makes it a true
rye whisky. Hirsch is one, and
connoisseurs claim it rivals the
best Kentucky ryes. The whiskies
are bottled in small batches, made
in column stills, aged in ex-
bourbon barrels, selected by
Preiss Imports, and bottled by
Glenora Distillers, Nova Scotia,
which also produces a single malt
called Glen Breton (*see p128*).

◄ HIRSCH SELECTION 8-YEAR-OLD

CANADIAN RYE 43% ABV
Solvent and pine essence, then sweet
maple sap on the nose. The taste is
sweet, with caramel, dry coconut, and
oak; full-bodied. A bittersweet finish
with a few earthy notes.

HIRSCH RESERVE

US

Distribution: Preiss Imports

Hirsch Reserve is a drop of US whiskey history. The spirit itself was distilled in 1974 at Michter's Distillery, the last surviving one in Pennsylvania. Michter's closed in 1988, but one Adolf H. Hirsch had acquired a considerable stock of the spirit some years previously and, after it had been matured for 16 years, it was put into stainless steel tanks to prevent further aging. This whiskey is now available from Preiss Imports but, once gone, is gone forever.

HIRSCH RESERVE ▶
BOURBON 45.8% ABV
Caramel, honey, and rye dominate the complex nose, with a whiff of smoke also coming through. Oily corn, honey, and oak on the rich palate, with rye and more oak in the drying finish.

181

HOLLE

Switzerland

Hollen 52, 4426 Lauwil, Basel
www.swiss-whisky.ch

Until July 1, 1999, it was strictly forbidden in Switzerland to distill spirit from grain, which was considered a food staple. After a change in the law, the Bader family, who had been making fruit spirits for a long time, started to distill from grains, and became the country's first whisky producer.

On label:
> 742
> Holle
> Single Malt
> Swiss Whisky
>
> Seit 1999
>
> Familie Bader, Holle, 4426 Lauwil
> Tel. 061 941 15 41. Fax 061 943 10 27
> www.swiss-whisky.ch
>
> 42% Vol   Gerstenmalz   70 cl

◀ **HOLLE**

SINGLE MALT 42% ABV

Delicate aromas of malt, wood, and vanilla, with a flavor of wine. There are two varieties: one is matured in a white-wine cask, the other in a red-wine cask. A cask strength version is bottled at 51.1% ABV.

HUDSON

US

Tuthilltown Distillery, 14 Gristmill Lane, Gardiner, New York
www.tuthilltown.com

In 1825, New York State had more than 1,000 working distilleries and produced a major share of the nation's whiskey. These days, Tuthilltown is New York's only remaining distillery. It was founded in 2001 by Brian Lee and Ralph Erenzo, and produces a quartet of "Hudson" bottlings, including a rich and full-flavored four-grain whiskey and a rich, caramel single malt, intended as an American "re-interpretation" of traditional Scottish whiskies.

HUDSON MANHATTAN RYE ▶

RYE WHISKEY 46% ABV

The first whiskey to be distilled in New York State for more than 80 years. Floral notes and a smooth finish on the palate, with a recognizable rye edge.

HUDSON BABY BOURBON

BOURBON 46% ABV

Made with 100 percent New York State corn, this is the first bourbon ever to be made in New York. It is a mildly sweet, smooth spirit with subtle hints of vanilla and caramel.

I.W. HARPER

US

Four Roses Distillery,
1224 Bond Mills Road,
Lawrenceburg, Kentucky
www.fourroses.us

The historic and once bestselling
I.W. Harper brand was established
by Jewish businessman Isaac
Wolfe Bernheim (1848–1945),
a major figure in the bourbon
business at the turn of the
20th century.

It was made at the Bernheim
Distillery (*see p48*) in Louisville.
It is now produced for current
owners Diageo by Four Roses
Distillery and is one of the leading
bourbons in the Japanese market.

◀ **I.W. HARPER**
BOURBON 41% ABV
A big-bodied bourbon in which pepper
combines with mint, oranges, caramel,
and quite youthful charring on the
nose, while caramel, apples, and oak
feature on the elegant palate. The
finish is dry and smoky.

ICHIRO'S MALT

Japan
Hanyu Distillery, Saitama Prefecture
www.one-drinks.com

Ichiro's Malt is a range of bottlings from Ichiro Akuto, who was the former president of Hanyu *(see p172)*, and the grandson of the founder Isouji Akuto. The whiskies are drawn from the 400 casks of Hanyu single malt that Akuto managed to obtain after the Hanyu distillery was closed down.

The bulk of Hanyu's remaining stock is being released by Akuto in a series of 53 whiskies named after playing cards. This Card Series, ☞

ICHIRO'S MALT & GRAIN ▶
SINGLE MALT 46% ABV
Honey, vanilla, malt, and apricots on the nose. The palate offers more honey, plus citrus fruit, ginger, pepper, and sweet hay. Tropical fruits in the peppery finish.

ICHIRO'S MALT—ACE OF DIAMONDS, DISTILLED 1986, BOTTLED 2008
SINGLE MALT 56.4% ABV
Mature nose, with Seville orange, furniture polish, rose, pipe tobacco, and when diluted, sloe and Moscatel. Spicy and chocolatey on the tongue.

ICHIRO'S MALT

as it is known, is memorable not only for its distinctive branding but also for the high quality of many of its expressions.

Distillation dates for the Card Series range from 1985 to 2000, with some of the expressions being given secondary maturation in other types of barrel, Japanese oak and sherry among them. All of the Card Series bottlings are now extremely rare and highly collectible.

◀ ICHIRO'S MALT DOUBLE DISTILLERIES

BLENDED MALT 46% ABV

The nose is sweet and oaky, with sawdust and hints of sandalwood. Malt and spice on the palate, with developing oak and licorice.

ICHIRO'S MALT—ACE OF SPADES, DISTILLED 1985, BOTTLED 2006

SINGLE MALT 55% ABV

Sometimes called the Motorhead malt, after the band who sang *Ace of Spades*, this is one of the oldest in the Card Series. Bold, rich, and fat with masses of raisin, some tarry notes, and treacle. The palate is chewy and toffeelike, with some prune and a savory finish.

IMPERIAL BLUE

India
Owner: Pernod Ricard
www.pernod-ricard.com

Imperial Blue is Pernod Ricard's
second bestselling brand in India,
at over 3.8 million cases a year.
Previously a Seagram's brand (and
still labeled as such), it benefited
hugely from Pernod Ricard's
acquisition of Seagram in 2001,
jumping from producing under
half a million cases to over a
million by 2002. Imperial Blue hit
the headlines in 2008 when some
bottles in Andhra Pradesh were
found to be understrength. It later
transpired that they had been
sabotaged by disgruntled workers.

IMPERIAL BLUE ▶

BLEND 42.8% ABV
In spite of the "grain" in its name,
Imperial Blue is a blend of imported
Scotch malt and locally made neutral
spirit. It is light, sweet, and smooth.

INCHGOWER

Scotland
Buckie, Banffshire
www.malts.com

This is Speyside, but only just—
the Inchgower Distillery sits near
the mouth of the Spey and the
fishing port of Buckie. It was
established in 1871 by Alexander
Wilson, using equipment from the
disused Tochieneal Distillery,
which had been founded in 1824
by his father, John Wilson, a short
distance down the coast at Cullen.
It remained a family business
until 1930, when the stills went
cold. Six years on, the local town
council bought it for just $4,970,
selling it on to Arthur Bell & Sons
in 1938. Bell's blends swallow
up most of the malt.

◀ INCHGOWER FLORA & FAUNA 14-YEAR-OLD
SINGLE MALT: SPEYSIDE 43% ABV
Brisk and fresh, with a floral nose,
sweet-and-sour flavor, developing
into a very short finish.

INVER HOUSE GREEN PLAID

Scotland
Owner: Inver House Distillers

Controlled today by Thai Beverage, Inver House is one of the smaller but more dynamic Scotch whisky companies and, in 2008, was named International Distiller of the Year by *Whisky Magazine*. Its Green Plaid label was originally launched in 1956 in the US, where it remains among the top ten best-selling whiskies. More than 20 malts and grains are used to blend Green Plaid, which is available as a competitively priced non-aged version and as 12- and 21-year-olds. Inver House's Speyburn, anCnoc, Balblair, Old Pulteney, and Balmenach single malts undoubtedly feature strongly in the blend.

INVER HOUSE GREEN PLAID ▶
BLEND 40% ABV
A light, pleasant, undemanding dram, with notes of caramel and vanilla.

INVERGORDON

Scotland

Cottage Brae, Invergordon, Ross-shire
www.whyteandmackay.com

Located on the shores of the
Moray Firth, the Invergordon
grain distillery is owned by Whyte
& Mackay. It was established in
1961 and expanded in 1963 and
1978. The distillery issued its
pioneering official bottling of
Invergordon Single Grain as a
10-year-old in 1991, but this was
subsequently withdrawn. As a
consequence, the only supplies
now available are independent
bottlings, many of which are
very highly regarded by
independent tasters.

◀ INVERGORDON CLAN DENNY 1966

SINGLE GRAIN 49.8% ABV
The independent bottlings of
Invergordon are uniformly old
(typically 38–42 years), and are
characterized by a sweet nose and
creamy texture. Expect notes of
vanilla and wood, and spices such
as cinnamon and nutmeg.

THE IRISHMAN

Ireland
Walsh Whiskey Distillery
Royal Oak, County Carlow
www.irishmanwhiskey.com

The Irishman whiskey was launched in 2007 by Bernard and Rosemary Walsh, who had previously specialized in bottling an Irish coffee recipe under the Hot Irishman label. The range now includes the Single Malt, the Founder's Reserve, and The Irishman Rare Cask Strength.

THE IRISHMAN FOUNDER'S RESERVE ▶
BLEND 40% ABV

Cooking apples, vanilla, and black pepper on the nose. Rich mouthfeel, with cinnamon, peaches, caramel, and spicy oak.

THE IRISHMAN SINGLE MALT
SINGLE MALT 40% ABV

Bushmills tends to keep all the best whiskey for itself, which means the Irishman malt has great cereal character but will never be anything outstanding. There is a hint of sherry on the palate.

ISLAY MIST

Ireland
Owner: MacDuff International

Created in 1922 for the 21st birthday of the son of the Laird of Islay House, Islay Mist is a highly awarded blend of single malts from the Hebridean island. The strongly flavored Laphroaig is predominant, but is tempered with Speyside and Highland malts. Naturally, Islay Mist is favored by lovers of peat-flavored whiskies, but it also offers an excellent alternative to less characterful blends. It is produced by MacDuff International, and is available in Peated Reserve, Deluxe, 12-, and 17-year-old.

◀ ISLAY MIST DELUXE
BLEND 40% ABV

A great smoky session whisky that some will find easier to drink than full-on Islay malt. Sweet and complex under all the peat.

Deluxe

ISLAY MIST

Blended
SCOTCH WHISKY

DISTILLED, BLENDED &
BOTTLED IN SCOTLAND
MACDUFF INTERNATIONAL

WHISKEYS

I

GREAT

J&B

Scotland
Owner: Diageo

A Diageo brand widely sold in Spain, France, Portugal, Turkey, South Africa, and the US, J&B is one of the world's top-selling blended whiskies.

The founding firm dates from 1749. In 1831 it was bought by the entrepreneurial Alfred Brooks, who renamed it Justerini and Brooks. The company began blending in the 1880s, and developed J&B Rare in the 1930s, when the end of Prohibition in the US created a demand for lighter-colored whisky with a more delicate flavor.

J&B RARE ▶
BLEND 40% ABV
Top-class single malts such as Knockando, Auchroisk, and Glen Spey are at its heart; delicate smokiness suggests an Islay influence. Apple and pear sweetness, vanilla, and honey hint against a background of restrained peat.

J&B JET
BLEND 40% ABV
A very mellow, smooth whisky, with Speyside malt at its core.

JACK DANIEL'S

US

*280 Lynchburg Road,
Lynchburg, Tennessee
www.jackdaniels.com*

Jack Daniel's has become an iconic brand worldwide. Its founder, Jasper Newton "Jack" Daniel reputedly started to make whiskey as a child, and by 1860 was running his own distilling business at the tender age of 14.

Today, Jack Daniel's is owned by the Kentucky-based Brown-Forman Corporation.

◀ JACK DANIEL'S OLD NO. 7
TENNESSEE WHISKEY 40% ABV
Powerful nose of vanilla, smoke, and licorice. On the palate, oily cough-mixture and molasses, with a final kick of maple syrup and burnt wood lingering in the finish. Not particularly complex, but muscular and distinctive.

JACK DANIEL'S SINGLE BARREL
TENNESSEE WHISKEY 47% ABV
Charming and smooth on the nose, with notes of peach, vanilla, nuts, and oak. The comparatively dry palate offers depth, richness, and elegance, with oily corn, licorice, malt, and oak. Malt and oak linger in the lengthy finish, along with a touch of rye spice.

JAMES MARTIN'S

Scotland
Owner: Glenmorangie

The James Martin name relates to the Leith blenders MacDonald Martin Distillers (now Glenmorangie,) and dates back to 1878, when the original James Martin set up in business. Presented in stylish Art Deco bottles, the blend was always highly regarded, as it contained a healthy share of Glenmorangie single malt with some richer components.

Currently there are 12- and 20-year-old versions of James Martin's, while bottles of the 30-year-old can still be bought from specialist retailers.

JAMES MARTIN'S 20-YEAR-OLD ▶
BLEND 40% ABV

Citrus on the nose initially, then honey, vanilla, and a rich mead liqueur. With water, hints of coconut and vanilla appear. Very soft on the palate at the start, with cereal (grain) notes to the fore. Complex, lively spice and soft, sweet grain notes. Well-balanced with a soft finish.

JAMESON

Ireland

*Midleton Distillery,
Midleton, County Cork*
www.jamesonwhiskey.com

This is the biggest-selling Irish whiskey. The standard blend is a 50:50 blend of medium-bodied pot still and grain whiskey. It's a light spirit that lacks character. Beyond the standard bottling, though, are some cracking whiskeys. Gold Reserve was originally launched as a premium, duty-free blend, but it is now widely available. Some of the whiskeys used in it are more

◄ JAMESON STANDARD BLEND
BLEND 40% ABV

The malty smell is promising, but the drink itself is a let-down. The grain is unruly and overwhelms the pot still, leaving some citrus notes. There is a gentle buzz of sherry—nothing more.

JAMESON GOLD RESERVE
BLEND 43% ABV

This is a viscous, oily, syrupy mouth-coater of a whiskey. Finer, lighter flavors find it hard to fight their way through the fug of sugars. The finish is buzzy and long, in rather the same way as a cough medicine.

than 20 years old, but they are cut with younger pot still whiskey, matured in first-fill oak casks. This is the only Irish whiskey to feature virgin wood, giving the blend a sweet, vanillalike flavor.

Jameson's Special Reserve 12-year-old stays in Oloroso sherry butts for 12 years and has won several awards. Six extra years in the cask doesn't change the flavor profile of the 18-year-old premium offering much, but it does double the price.

JAMESON SPECIAL RESERVE 12-YEAR-OLD ▶

BLEND 40% ABV

A world-beating whiskey. Hints of leather and spice on the nose and an incredibly silky quality in the mouth. Dried fruits wrapped in milk chocolate round off a master-class in how to make a great whiskey.

JAMESON LIMITED RESERVE 18-YEAR-OLD

BLEND 40% ABV

The pot still here has taken old age well. The body is firm and yielding and the Oloroso wood has to be very fine not to dominate a blend this old. Sweet almond and spiced fudge notes complement the oiliness of the pot still.

Whiskey Tour:
IRELAND

In 1887, when the Victorian travel and drinks writer Alfred Barnard visited Ireland, he had 28 different distilleries to visit. Nowadays, the range is more limited, but every bit as enjoyable. Several historic whiskey distilleries have facilities for tourists, and there are other attractions and the beautiful Irish landscape to explore.

DAY 1: GIANTS CAUSEWAY, BUSHMILLS

❶ Start your trip at the magnificent **Giants Causeway**, a World Heritage Site near the town of Bushmills, where extraordinary hexagonal basalt columns stretch out along the rugged coast.

❷ Of all the Irish distilleries that are open to the public, **Bushmills** is the only one that is still in production. Enjoy the tour, sample some fine whiskeys, then stay at the nearby Bushmills Inn for some great food and a good night's sleep.

GIANTS CAUSEWAY

DAY 2: COOLEY, OLD JAMESON DISTILLERY

COOLEY DISTILLERY

❸ Although **Cooley** Distillery is not open to the public, the nearby hills and the seaside town of Greenore are worth seeing on the way to Dublin.

❹ Avoid the Dublin traffic by taking the LUAS tram from Junction 9 of the M50 to Smithfield in the city center. This is near the **Old Jameson Distillery**, which offers guided tours and the chance to sample Jameson whiskey.

miles
0   25

0   25
kilometers

N56

N15
N16

N59

N5

N4

N17

N63

N59

○ GALWAY

N6

N18

N7

LIMERICK ○

N69

N21

N20

N8

N72

FINISH

N70

N22

CORK **❼** **❽**
THE JAMESON
EXPERIENCE

N71

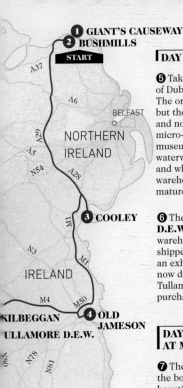

① GIANT'S CAUSEWAY
② BUSHMILLS
START

A37

A6

BELFAST

NORTHERN
IRELAND

A29
A5
N54
A28

M1

③ COOLEY

N3

IRELAND

M1

M4
M50

**④ OLD
JAMESON**

N80

KILBEGGAN
ULLAMORE D.E.W.

N78
N81

N9
N11

24
N25   WATERFORD

TOUR STATISTICS

DAYS: 4
LENGTH: 375 miles (600km)
TRAVEL: Car, tram, walking
DISTILLERIES: 1 working,
3 converted

DAY 3: KILBEGGAN, TULLAMORE D.E.W.

⑤ Take Junction 7 of the M50 and head west out of Dublin to the old Locke's building at **Kilbeggan**. The original distillery fell silent in 1957, but the site has been revived by locals and now houses the Kilbeggan micro-distillery and a whiskey museum with working waterwheel, restaurant, shop, and whiskey bar. Cooley leases warehouses at this site and matures some whiskeys here.

KILBEGGAN

⑥ The vibrant town of Tullamore is home to the **Tullamore D.E.W.** visitor center. This building used to be a bonded warehouse for storing whiskey casks before they were shipped downstream to Dublin, and is now the setting for an exhibition about traditional whiskey making. Although now distilled at Clonminch, on the outskirts of the town, Tullamore whiskey is, of course, available for tasting and purchase at the visitor center.

DAY 4: CORK, THE JAMESON EXPERIENCE AT MIDLETON

⑦ The cross-country trip from Tullamore to Cork traverses the boggy heart of Ireland—a bleak landscape that is strangely beautiful at any time of the year. **Cork** city is a food haven, where you can visit the historic English Market to buy a picnic lunch, or perhaps try the Market Café for local specialties. For a drink, stop at the South County Bar & Café, in Douglas Village, a suburb of Cork. It's a traditional pub with its own "whiskey corner" to celebrate Irish whiskey.

POT STILL AT MIDLETON

⑧ **The Jameson Experience** is set in the beautifully restored 18th-century distillery at Midleton, and boasts the world's largest pot still, which now stands outside the buildings. For refreshment, try the restaurant at nearby Ballymaloe House, which is overseen by Darina Allen, the doyen of Irish foodies.

JEFFERSON'S

US

*McLain & Kyne Ltd. (Castle Brands),
Louisville, Kentucky
www.mclainandkyne.com*

The Louisville company of McLain
& Kyne, Ltd. was formed by Trey
Zoeller to carry on the distilling
traditions of his ancestors. McLain
& Kyne specializes in premium,
very small-batch bourbons, most
notably Jefferson's and Sam
Houston (*see p309*).

◄ JEFFERSON'S SMALL BATCH 8-YEAR-OLD

BOURBON (VARIABLE ABV)

This bourbon has been aged in the
heart of metal-clad warehouses to
accentuate the extreme temperatures
of Kentucky, forcing the bourbon to
expand deep into the barrel and
extract desirable flavors from the
wood. The nose is fresh, with vanilla
and ripe peach notes, while the
smooth, sweet palate boasts more
vanilla, caramel, and berries. The
finish is very delicate, with toasted
vanilla and cream.

JIM BEAM

US

Jim Beam Distillery, 149 Happy Hollow Road, Clermont, Kentucky
www.jimbeam.com

Jim Beam is the best-selling bourbon brand in the world, and its origins date back to the 18th century, when German-born farmer and miller Jacob Boehm traveled west into Bourbon County, Kentucky, from Virginia, carrying with him his copper pot still. He is reputed to have sold his first barrel of whiskey for cash in 1795, and subsequently moved his distilling operation into ☞

JIM BEAM WHITE LABEL 4-YEAR-OLD ▶

BOURBON 40% ABV
Vanilla and delicate floral notes on the nose. Initially sweet, with restrained vanilla, then drier, oaky notes develop, fading into furniture polish and soft malt in the finish

JIM BEAM BLACK LABEL 6-YEAR-OLD

BOURBON 43% ABV
The nose offers caramel, vanilla, and ripe oranges, while the palate is smooth, with honey, fudge, and citrus fruits.

JIM BEAM

 Washington County when he inherited land there.

Jim (James Beauregard) Beam himself was Jacob Boehm's great-grandson. He joined the family business at the age of 16, in 1880, and trade prospered in the years before Prohibition forced the closure of the distillery.

Jim Beam founded the present Clermont Distillery soon after the repeal of Prohibition in 1933, despite being 70 years old at the time. He died in 1947, five years after "Jim Beam" first appeared on the bottle label, and two years after the firm had been sold to Harry Blum of Chicago, previously a partner in the company.

◀ JIM BEAM DEVIL'S CUT
BOURBON 45% ABV

Freshly planed wood and spicy vanilla on the nose, with vanilla and oak majoring on the palate, plus more vanilla and spice.

JIM BEAM RYE
RYE WHISKEY 40% ABV

Light, perfumed, and aromatic on the nose, with lemon and mint. Oily in the mouth, with soft fruits, honey, and rye. Drying and spicy in the finish.

JOHNNIE WALKER

Scotland
Owner: Diageo

While the original firm can be traced back to the purchase of a Kilmarnock grocery store in 1820, Walker's (as it was then known) did not enter the whisky business in a serious way until the 1860s. Then, John Walker's son and grandson progressively launched and developed their range of whiskies. These were based around the original Walker's Old Highland blend, which was launched in 1865 and is the ☞

JOHNNIE WALKER BLACK LABEL ▶

BLEND 40% ABV

The flagship, classic blend, recognizable by the smoky kick contributed by Talisker, Caol Ila, and Lagavulin. Glendullan and Mortlach add some Speyside malt.

JOHNNIE WALKER GREEN LABEL

BLENDED MALT 43% ABV

Complex, rich, and powerful. Pepper and oak, fruit aromas, a malty sweetness, and some smoke.

JOHNNIE WALKER

 ancestor of today's Black Label. In 1925 the firm joined DCL and, by 1945, the newly renamed "Johnnie Walker" was the world's bestselling brand of Scotch.

The range comprises Johnnie Walker Red, Black, Double Black, Gold, Platinum, and Blue. From time to time the firm also releases one-off, limited, or regional expressions. From the early 1990s, the brand positioned itself upmarket. Blue Label, launched in 1992, set new price records for blended whisky. The King George V Edition followed, costing three times more than the Blue, then the ultra-exclusive 1805, sold at $1,300 a glass.

◄ JOHNNIE WALKER GOLD LABEL

BLEND 40% ABV

Honey, fresh fruit, and toffee notes, with smoke in the background. Diageo recommends chilling this in the freezer before serving.

JOHNNIE WALKER BLUE LABEL

BLEND 40% ABV

Smooth and mellow, with traces of spice, honey, and the signature hint of smoke.

JOHNNY DRUM

US

Kentucky Bourbon Distillers,
1869 Loretto Road,
Bardstown, Kentucky
www.kentuckybourbonwhiskey.com

Johnny Drum is said to have been a Confederate drummer boy during the Civil War, and later a pioneer farmer and distiller in Kentucky. Johnny Drum bourbon was formerly produced in the Willet Distillery near Bardstown, but this closed in the early 1980s when the last of the Willet family members retired. The plant was acquired by Kentucky Bourbon Distillers, Ltd., for whom a range of whiskeys is distilled under contract.

JOHNNY DRUM ▶
BOURBON (VARIABLE ABV)
Smooth and elegant on the nose, with vanilla, gentle spices, and smoke. This is a full-bodied bourbon, well-balanced and smooth in the mouth, with vanilla and a hint of smoke. The finish is lingering and sophisticated.

JURA

Scotland

Isle of Jura, Argyllshire
www.jurawhisky.com

When two estate owners on Jura resurrected the Jura distillery in the late 1950s, half a century after it had fallen into disuse, the profile of the whisky changed. Gone was the strong, phenolic malt of the past, and in came something more Highland in style, with less peat and a more subtle touch, although in recent years Jura has also produced an array of limited-edition bottlings, some of which have been quite heavily peated.

Jura's core range consists of 10-year-old, Origin, 16-year-old, Diurach's Own, Superstition, and the peated Prophecy.

◀ **JURA 10-YEAR-OLD**
SINGLE MALT: ISLANDS 40% ABV
A lightly peated island malt that seems to have improved in recent years.

JURA SUPERSTITION
SINGLE MALT: ISLANDS 43% ABV
A mix of heavily peated, young Jura with older whisky, to produce an intensely smoky, smooth-textured malt.

KENTUCKY GENTLEMAN

US

*Barton Distillery, 300 Barton Road,
Bardstown, Kentucky*
www.sazerac.com

Kentucky Gentleman is offered
both as a blended whiskey and as
a straight bourbon. According to
its producers, the blended version
is created from a blend of Kentucky
straight bourbon whiskey and
spirits from the finest grains.

The popular straight expression
enjoys a notably loyal following in
the southern states, particularly
Florida, Alabama, and Virginia.
Kentucky Gentleman is produced
in Bardstown, which was
controlled by Barton Brands until
2009, when it was sold to the New
Orleans-based Sazerac Company.

KENTUCKY GENTLEMAN ▶
BOURBON 40% ABV
Made with a higher percentage of rye
than most Barton whiskeys, this offers
caramel and sweet oak aromas, and
is oily, full-bodied, spicy, and fruity
in the mouth. Rye, fruits, vanilla, and
cocoa figure in the lingering, flavorful,
and comparatively assertive finish.

KESSLER

US

Jim Beam Distillery,
149 Happy Hollow Road,
Clermont, Kentucky
www.beamsuntory.com

One of the best-known and most highly regarded blended American whiskeys, Kessler traces its origins back to 1888, when it was first blended by one Julius Kessler, who traveled from saloon to saloon across the West, selling his whiskey as he went. Kessler Whiskey was acquired by The Seagram Company during the mid-1930s, eventually passing to Beam Inc., which was then purchased by Suntory Holdings in 2014. Kessler is now produced by Beam Suntory, and is the second-best-selling American blended whiskey.

◀ KESSLER

BLEND 40% ABV

Lives up to its "Smooth as silk" slogan. Light, fruity nose and sweet palate with enough complexity of licorice and leather achieved by the blend's four-year aging.

KILBEGGAN

Ireland

The Old Kilbeggan Distillery, Main Street, Kilbeggan, County Westmeath
www.kilbegganwhiskey.com

In the mid-1950s, the most famous of the distilleries, John Locke & Sons, fell silent. Although the two remaining Locke family members —sisters Flo and Sweet—had warehouses full of raw ingredients, they had no interest in whiskey-making. With post-war whiskey prices on the rise, they decided to sell the distillery.

Nowadays, Kilbeggan whiskeys are Cooley blends, distilled in County Louth, but the spirits are still matured and bottled on site.

KILBEGGAN ▶
BLEND 40% ABV

A grainy blend, with strong notes of honey and oatmeal. The end note is a pleasing combination of coffee and dark chocolate.

KILBEGGAN 15-YEAR-OLD
BLEND 40% ABV

Age can thin and fracture a whiskey, or it can be its making. The Kilbeggan 15-year-old blend is spectacular. Expect the usual Cooley honey and cookie notes, distilled to perfection.

KILCHOMAN

Scotland
Rockside Farm, Bruichladdich, Islay
www.kilchomandistillery.com

Whisky-making began here in 2005, and this is as quintessential a farm distillery as you'll find. The barley is grown on Rockside Farm, and malting, fermenting, distilling, and maturing all take place onsite; a dam on the farm creates a supply of fresh water.

Having started out selling new-make spirit, Kilchoman released its first 3-year-old single malt in 2009, followed by several limited bottlings before the first "core" expression—Machir Bay—appeared in 2012. Loch Gorm and 100% Islay are also regularly produced.

◀ KILCHOMAN MACHIR BAY
SINGLE MALT 46% ABV

A nose of sweet peat and vanilla, undercut by brine, wood smoke, kelp, and black pepper. Smooth on the palate, with citrus fruit, peat smoke, and antiseptic, leading to a long, sweet, chili and nut finish.

KILKERRAN

Scotland
Glengyle Road, Campbeltown
www.kilkerransinglemalt.com

The original Glengyle operated between 1872 and 1925, when Campbeltown was still a major player in the Scotch whisky world, and was reopened in 2004. The malt whisky it produces is named Kilkerran, as "Glengyle" was already registered as a blend by Loch Lomond. It is named after an early settlement that would later become Campbeltown.

The first permanent expression of Kilkerran will be a 12-year-old, but since 2009, the distillery has released annual limited batches of "Work in Progress." In 2014, "Work in Progress 6" featured both sherry cask–matured and bourbon cask–matured bottlings.

KILKERRAN WORK IN PROGRESS 6 BOURBON MATURED ▶

SINGLE MALT: CAMPBELTOWN
46% ABV

Lemongrass, a pinch of salt, wood smoke, and ginger snaps on the nose. Tropical fruits on the soft, oily palate, with a slight underpinning of nutty, spicy smoke. Drying in the mellow finish.

KIRIN GOTEMBA

Japan
Shibanta 970, Gotembashi, Shizuoka
www.kirin.co.jp

Kirin's Gotemba distillery was built in 1973 as part of a joint venture with the former Canadian giant Seagram (*see p310*). The distillery's output is much in line with the light flavors typical of Seagram's house style, which was also the style preferred by the Japanese consumer in the 1970s. That said, the distillery had to supply all the needs of Kirin's blends, so it made three different grain whiskies and three styles of malt, including peated.

◄ GOTEMBA FUJISANROKU 18-YEAR-OLD
SINGLE MALT 40% ABV
More floral and restrained than the "old" Fuji Gotemba 18-year-old, with less of the oakiness. Some peach, lily, and a zesty grapefruit note. The honey found in the grain reappears here.

FUJISANROKU TARUJUKU 50°
BLEND 50% ABV
Vanilla and light oak on the slightly spirit-y nose, while the palate is oaky, with malt and allspice, leading to a short finish.

KIRIN KARUIZAWA

Japan
Maseguchi 1795–2, Oaza, Miyotamachi, Kitasakugun, Nagano
www.kirin.co.jp

This former winery was converted to whisky-making in the 1950s. To get its big-hitting and smoky style, it retains techniques that are rare now even in Scotland: the heaviness of the Golden Promise strain of barley used is accentuated by the small stills, while maturation in ex-sherry casks adds a dried-fruit character.

KARUIZAWA 1995: NOH SERIES, BOTTLED 2008 ▶

SINGLE MALT 63% ABV

Hugely resinous nose that mixes tiger balm, geranium, boot polish, prune, and oiled woods. Lightly astringent palate that needs water to release the tannic grip. An exotic, floral whisky.

KNAPPOGUE CASTLE

Ireland

Bushmills Distillery, 2 Distillery Road, County Antrim

After World War II, the owner of Knappogue Castle took to buying casks of whiskey, which he would store in a cellar. These whiskeys would then be bottled and given away to family and friends over time. The last of these original casks, filled with Tullamore whiskey, was bottled in 1987.

In the 1990s the son of the castle's owner, Mark Andrews, decided to follow suit and bottle single vintages of his own, also labeled Knappogue Castle.

The first of these were created from whiskey produced at Cooley Distillery, but the more recent vintages come from Bushmills.

◀ KNAPPOGUE CASTLE 1995

SINGLE MALT 40% ABV

Clearly originates from a Bushmills malt, and a classy one to boot. There are notes of toasted nuts, while a juicy, honey sweetness lingers on the palate. It is still too young, though, to display the full potential of its characteristics.

KNOB CREEK

US

Jim Beam Distillery,
149 Happy Hollow Road,
Clermont, Kentucky
www.knobcreek.com

Knob Creek is the Kentucky
town where Abraham Lincoln's
father, Thomas, owned a farm
and worked at the local distillery.
This bourbon is one of three
introduced in 1992, when Jim
Beam launched its Small Batch
Bourbon Collection. It is made
to the same high-rye formula
as the Jim Beam–distilled Basil
Hayden's *(see p38)* and Old
Grand-Dad *(p270)* brands.

Several new bottles have been
added to the Knob Creek range
since its launch, including, in
2012, Knob Creek Straight Rye
Whiskey—the brand's first
expression not to carry an
age statement.

KNOB CREEK 9-YEAR-OLD ▶
BOURBON 50% ABV
Nutty nose of sweet, tangy fruit
and rye. Malt, spice, and nuts on the
fruity palate, drying finish with notes
of vanilla.

215

GREAT K WHISKEYS

KNOCKANDO

Scotland

Knockando, Morayshire
www.malts.com

Knockando was launched as a single malt in the late 1970s. Most of the distillery's production has tended to go into J&B.

Established in 1898, the distillery was only run on a seasonal basis and soon fell victim to the speculative crash that hit the industry at the beginning of the 20th century. Knockando was snapped up by the London gin distillers Gilbey's, who, via a series of acquisitions, became part of what is now Diageo. In 1968, the floor maltings were stopped and the old malt barns converted to host meetings for J&B salesmen.

◄ KNOCKANDO 12-YEAR-OLD
SINGLE MALT: SPEYSIDE 43% ABV
This gentle, grassy malt has a cereal character and a light, creamy texture.

KNOCKANDO 18-YEAR-OLD
SINGLE MALT: SPEYSIDE 43% ABV
A slightly more fulsome expression, with a smooth, mellow texture.

KNOCKEEN HILLS

Ireland
www.irish-poteen.com

Poteen (or poitín) is a clear spirit that was traditionally distilled in homemade pot stills throughout Ireland. It was first made with malted barley or any available grain, or sometimes potatoes.

One of the few to survive is Knockeen Hills. Its spirit is bottled at three strengths: triple-distilled at 60% and 70% ABV, and quadruple-distilled at 90% ABV. It should not be drunk neat.

KNOCKEEN HILLS POTEEN— FARMER'S STRENGTH ▶

POTEEN 60% ABV

Clean, fresh, and fruity on the nose. Creamy textured, with tantalizing sweet and juicy fruit notes on the palate. Crisp, mouth-cleansing finish.

KNOCKEEN HILLS POTEEN— GOLD STRENGTH

POTEEN 70% ABV

With a large measure of water (almost 50:50), it becomes fruity, with tangerine-skin aromas. Warming in the mouth, sweet and sour on the palate, with a dry, fruit-tinged finish.

LAGAVULIN

Scotland
Port Ellen, Isle of Islay
www.malts.com

Lagavulin is said to have evolved into a distillery from various illicit smuggling cottages in 1817. In 1836 its lease was taken over by Alexander Graham, who sold the island's whiskies through his shop in Glasgow. Peter Mackie, the nephew of Graham's partner, worked for the business and went on to create the famous White Horse blend based on Islay malt. When Laphroaig refused to supply him, he built Malt Mill Distillery in the grounds of Lagavulin—inherited after his uncle's death.

◀ LAGAVULIN 16-YEAR-OLD
SINGLE MALT: ISLAY 43% ABV
Intensely smoky nose with the scent of seaweed and iodine and a sweetness in the mouth that dries to a peaty finish.

LAGAVULIN 12-YEAR-OLD
SINGLE MALT: ISLAY 56.4% ABV
An initial sweetness gives way to scented smoke and a malty, fruity flavor ahead of the dry, peaty finish.

Malt Mill was demolished in the 1960s, but Lagavulin rode on the back of the White Horse until its iconic 16-year-old became a founding member of the "Classic Malts" in 1988.

During the slump in demand for Scotch in the 1980s, Lagavulin was working a two- to three-day week. Sixteen years down the line, the managers were having to juggle the short supply with booming demand. To try and meet demand, production at Lagavulin was cranked up to a seven-day week, and less and less was made available for blends. It is said that over 85 percent of Lagavulin is now bottled as a single malt.

LAGAVULIN DISTILLERS EDITION ▶

SINGLE MALT: ISLAY 43% ABV
A richer, fuller-flavored take on the 16-year-old, still with plenty of dense smoke and seaweed.

LAGAVULIN 21-YEAR-OLD

SINGLE MALT: ISLAY 56.5% ABV
Pungent and smoky on one hand, a sherried, syrupy warmth on the other. The two sides live in harmony.

LAMMERLAW

New Zealand
Bottled by Cadenhead
www.wmcadenhead.com

In 1974, the Wilson Brewery and
Malt Extract Company produced
New Zealand's first legal whisky
for 100 years. Unfortunately, its
pot stills were made from stainless
steel, and the spirit was horrible.
In 1981, the distillery was acquired
by Seagram, who vastly improved
quality and produced a 10-year-old
single malt—Lammerlaw—named
after the nearby mountain range.
The distillery was dismantled in
2002, and the casks passed to
Milford's owners (*see p251*).
Cadenhead has bottled Lammerlaw
in its World Whiskies series.

◀ CADENHEAD'S LAMMERLAW 10-YEAR-OLD
SINGLE MALT 47.3% ABV
Light-bodied and somewhat "green"
and cereal-like, but pleasant to taste.

LANGS

Scotland
Owner: Ian MacLeod
www.ianmacleod.com

At the heart of this blend is
Glengoyne single malt, from the
distillery outside Glasgow. This
was bought in 1876 by two local
merchants, Alexander and Gavin
Lang. Brand and distillery were
later sold to Robertson & Baxter.

The subsequent sale to Ian
MacLeod marked an important
transition for that business, from
blender and bottler to distiller.
Today, the principal Langs
products are Langs Select
12-year-old and Langs Supreme.

LANGS SUPREME ▶
BLEND 40% ABV

A rich malt aroma on the nose,
well matured, with just a hint of sherry.
A full-flavored, medium-sweet blend,
with the Glengoyne heart evident.

LANGS SELECT 12-YEAR-OLD
BLEND 40% ABV

Rhubarb, cooking apples, and plenty
of vanilla on the nose. Richer on the
palate, with lots of fruity notes and a
lemon-tart sweetness that build toward
a spicy finish with hints of peat smoke.

221

L

LAPHROAIG

Scotland
Port Ellen, Isle of Islay
www.laphroaig.com

Laphroaig has always reveled in its pungent smokiness—a mix of hemp, carbolic soap, and bonfire that is about as far from the creamy, cocktail end of whisky as it is possible to get. Its intense medicinal character is said to be one reason it was among the few Scotch whiskies allowed into the US during Prohibition—it was accepted as a "medicinal spirit," and could be obtained with a prescription from a doctor.

◀ LAPHROAIG 10-YEAR-OLD CASK STRENGTH

SINGLE MALT: ISLAY 57.3% ABV
Tar, seaweed, and salt, and some sweet wood, too. Iodine and hot peat rumble through a long, dramatic finish.

LAPHROAIG 10-YEAR-OLD

SINGLE MALT: ISLAY 40% ABV
The 10-year-old is also very popular. Beneath the dense peat smoke and salty sea spray is a refreshing, youthful malt with a sweet core.

Laphroaig was founded in 1810 by Alexander and Donald Johnston, although official production did not begin for five years. Living beside the equally famous Lagavulin has not always been easy, and there were the usual fights over water access, but today the feeling is more one of mutual respect.

Laphroaig is one of the very few distilleries to have retained its floor maltings, which supply about a fifth of its needs.

Quarter Cask is now offered alongside 10-year-old, 10-year-old Cask Strength, select, Triple Wood, and 18- and 25-year-old expressions.

LAPHROAIG QUARTER CASK ▶

SINGLE MALT: ISLAY 48% ABV
The Quarter Cask is at the heart of Laphroaig's core range. Small casks speed up the maturation process and lead to a sweet, woody taste that succumbs to a triumphal burst of peat smoke.

LAPHROAIG 25-YEAR-OLD

SINGLE MALT: ISLAY 50.9% ABV
A spicy, floral character, with smoke and sea spray taking over only in the finish. Also available in cask strength.

LARK

Australia

14 Davey Street, Hobart, Tasmania
www.larkdistillery.com

The modern revival of whisky-making in Australia began in Tasmania, with the opening of this small distillery in Hobart in 1992. It was the brainchild of Bill Lark, who realized that the island has all the right ingredients: plenty of rich barley fields; abundant pure, soft water; peat bogs; and a perfect climate for maturation.

Lark is now assisted by his wife Lyn and daughter Kristy. They use locally grown Franklin barley, 50 percent of it re-dried over peat. The malt is bottled from single casks at three to five years.

◄ LARK'S SINGLE MALT

SINGLE MALT 58% ABV
Malty and lightly peated, with peppery notes. A smooth mouthfeel, with rich malt, apples, and oak, and some spice in the finish.

LARK'S PM

BLENDED MALT 45% ABV
Sweet and smoky on the nose and palate; clean and lightly spicy. Consider this a well-made "barley schnapps."

THE LAST DROP

Scotland
www.lastdropdistillers.com

This unusual super-premium blend is the brainchild of three industry veterans—Tom Jago, James Espey, and Peter Fleck. Allegedly, a random discovery of very old whiskies pre-vatted at 12 years of age and then allowed to mature for a further 36 years in sherry casks, The Last Drop would appear to have been something of an accident and cannot be repeated. Included in the blend are whiskies from long-lost distilleries, the youngest reputed to have been distilled in 1960. Savor the tasting notes—at $1,300 or so a bottle, and with only 1,347 bottles available, it may be the closest you'll get to tasting it.

THE LAST DROP ▶
BLEND 54.5% ABV
Exceptionally complex nose, with figs, chocolate, and vanilla. An unusual combination of new-mown hay, dried fruit, herbs, and butter cookies.

LAUDER'S

Scotland
Owner: MacDuff International

Between 1886 and 1893, Lauder's Royal Northern Cream scooped up a total of six gold medals in international competitions—a tribute to the meticulous research and repeated trials undertaken by the original proprietor, Archibald Lauder, a Glasgow publican. The development of the blend is said to have taken him two years. Today Lauder's is once again blended in Glasgow, by MacDuff International, and Lauder's Bar on Sauchiehall Street remains to commemorate Lauder himself. His blend has largely slipped from public view in its homeland, but is imported by Barton Brands of Chicago to the US, where it remains popular among value-conscious consumers.

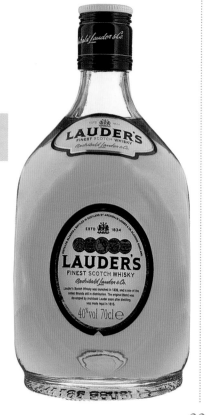

◀ **LAUDER'S**
BLEND 40% ABV
A light and fruity blend designed for session drinking and mixing.

LEDAIG

Scotland
Tobermory Distillery,
Tobermory, Isle of Mull

Tobermory, the capital of Mull and the island's main port, was originally called Ledaig, and this was the name chosen by John Sinclair when he began distilling here in 1798. When the Ledaig Distillery became Tobermory is unclear, as it has had an incredibly interrupted life, spending more time in mothballs than in production. In recent years the distillery adopted a similar approach to Springbank, producing a heavily peated robust West Coast malt called Ledaig and a lightly peated malt called Tobermory. At present 10- and 18-year-old expressions of Ledaig are available, along with 10- and 15-year-old Tobermorys *(see p347).*

LEDAIG 10-YEAR-OLD ▶
SINGLE MALT: ISLANDS 46.3% ABV
Slightly medicinal, but full of dry, somewhat dusty peat smoke.

LIMEBURNERS

Australia

*Great Southern Distilling Company,
252 Frenchman Bay Road, Albany,
Western Australia
www.distillery.com.au*

The Great Southern Distillery was
built in 2007, the brainchild of
lawyer and accountant Cameron
Syme. Its location was chosen for
Albany's cool, wet winters and
enough breeze to provide 75
percent of its energy needs by
wind power. It is close to the
Margaret River wineries, which
supply the ingredients for
schnapps and liqueur-making.
Limeburners whisky is offered
in single barrel bottlings: the
first, M2, launched in April 2008,
won an award.

◄ LIMEBURNERS BARREL M11
SINGLE MALT 43% ABV

The fourth bottling (M11), nicknamed
"The Dark One," is from a French oak
ex-brandy cask, re-racked into a
second-fill ex-bourbon barrel.

LINKWOOD

Scotland
Elgin, Morayshire
www.malts.com

From the outset, Linkwood was a well-conceived distillery. It was surrounded by barley fields to supply the grain and cattle to feed on the spent draff. The building you see today dates back to the 1870s, when the original Linkwood was demolished and a new distillery was built on the same site. Between 2011 and 2013, much of the existing distillery was demolished and replaced with new structures housing six stills.

LINKWOOD FLORA & FAUNA 12-YEAR-OLD ▶
SINGLE MALT: SPEYSIDE 43% ABV
On the lighter side of the Speyside style, with a fresh, grassy, green-apple fragrance and faint notes of spice. In the mouth it has a delicate sweet-and-sour flavor and a slow finish.

LINKWOOD RARE MALTS 26-YEAR-OLD
SINGLE MALT: SPEYSIDE 56.1% ABV
Bright and breezy for a 26-year-old. Lightly smoky with caramelized sugar notes. Spicy and warm in the finish.

LOCH FYNE

Scotland

Owner: The Whisky Shop
www.lochfynewhiskies.com

Created by Professor Ronnie Martin, a former production director at United Distillers (now Diageo), Loch Fyne is the exclusive and eponymous house blend of Loch Fyne Whiskies of Inverary. It is blended and bottled under license for this famous Scottish whisky specialist.

Slightly sweet and smoky, Loch Fyne is an easy-drinking, well-flavored blend, which has been praised by leading critics and won awards in international competition. Also available is a full-strength 12-year-old liqueur.

◄ LOCH FYNE PREMIUM SCOTCH

BLEND 40% ABV

Apple dumplings on the nose, enlivened by orange and tangerine notes. Subtle, with nutty, oil-related aromas and hints of smoke. The palate is smooth and well-balanced: acidic, salty, sweet, and dry. The finish is surprisingly warming.

LOCH LOMOND

Scotland
Alexandria, Dumbartonshire
www.lochlomonddistillery.com

Within the confines of the
Loch Lomond Distillery, on the
southern end of Loch Lomond,
all manner of Scotch whiskies
are produced, although originally
it was just malt. The distillery
was built in 1965 as a joint
venture between Barton Brands
of the US and Duncan Thomas.
Twenty years later it was bought
by Alexander Bulloch and his
company, Glen Catrine Bonded
Warehouse, Ltd, and is now owned
by Exponent Private Equity.
Today, grain whisky is produced
alongside the malt. The distillery's
stills have rectifying columns that
can be adjusted to produce a
lighter or heavier spirit.

LOCH LOMOND ▶
SINGLE MALT: HIGHLANDS 40% ABV
With no age statement and a
competitive price, this is likely to
be a fairly young single malt. It has
a light, fresh flavor and no great
influence of wood.

Locke's
AGED 8 YEARS
'SINGLE MALT'
PURE POT STILL
Irish Whiskey
1757
ESTABLISHED 1757
John Locke & Co. Ltd
40% Vol.
70cle

LOCKE'S

Ireland

Cooley Distillery, Riverstown, Cooley, County Louth
www.cooleywhiskey.com

It's hard to believe that, just 30 years ago, this amazing distillery was almost derelict. Since the early 1950s, when the Locke's whiskey business first folded, the abandoned distillery buildings had been used to house pigs and farm machinery. Then, in the late 1970s, the local community got together and restored the distillery. After the renovation was completed, a deal was made with Cooley and, after decades of dusty silence, whiskey barrels once more appeared in the warehouses.

◄ LOCKE'S 8-YEAR-OLD MALT

SINGLE MALT 40% ABV

A vatting of Cooley's unpeated malt, with a top dressing of peated malt. It is not a bad whiskey; just a bit dull.

LOCKE'S BLEND

BLEND 40% ABV

This is a pleasant enough dram. It would be particularly good in a hot whiskey, where its limited range doesn't have to sing out.

LONG JOHN

Scotland
Owner: Chivas Brothers

Despite reasonably healthy sales
in France, Scandinavia, and some
Spanish-speaking markets, Long
John appears very much the poor
relation in the Chivas Brothers'
stable, dominated as it is by
Chivas Regal and Ballantine's.
The brand has passed through
a number of owners since it was
founded in the early 19th century
by the eponymous "Long" John
MacDonald. In the past, Long
John has produced and marketed
12- and 15-year-old expressions,
but today, the concentration is on
the standard non-age version.

LONG JOHN 12-YEAR-OLD ▶
BLEND 40% ABV
A deluxe blend, Long John 12-year-old
is a dark, traditional style of whisky,
noted for its distinctive character. The
blend is said to contain 48 different
malts, including Laphroaig and
Highland Park.

233

LONGMORN

Scotland
Elgin, Morayshire

John Duff, George Thomson, and Charles Shirres went into partnership in 1894 and built the Longmorn distillery. With its four stills, it was conceived on a grand scale at a cost of $98,000 (around $3 million in today's money). Within five years Duff had bought out his partners and built another distillery, BenRiach, next door.

Now owned by Chivas Brothers, in 2012, Longmorn underwent major expansion work, with capacity extended to 990,000 gallons (4.5 million liters) per year.

◀ LONGMORN 16-YEAR-OLD
SINGLE MALT: SPEYSIDE 48% ABV
Its cereal aroma is sweetened with coconut from aging in bourbon casks. The mouthfeel is smooth and silky and dries on the tongue to give a crisp, slightly austere finish.

LONGMORN CASK STRENGTH
SINGLE MALT: SPEYSIDE 56.9% ABV
The nose is floral, with rose water, soft toffee, lemon, and sweet oak. Rich on the palate; creamy and sweet in the finish.

LONGROW

Scotland

Springbank Distillery,
Well Close, Campbeltown, Argyll
www.springbankdistillers.com

In 1973, the Springbank Distillery decided to distill a pungent, heavily smoked whisky alongside its main malt. The new whisky was christened Longrow after a distillery that had once stood next door. It was released as an experiment in 1985 and finally became a regular fixture in 1992.

Today, the core range includes Longrow, Red, and 18-year-old, the last released in small amounts from time to time.

LONGROW PEATED ▶

SINGLE MALT: CAMPBELTOWN
46% ABV

The nose offers vanilla, brine, and peat smoke, while the palate features early orchard fruits and milk chocolate before more brine and smoke appear.

LONGROW 18-YEAR-OLD

SINGLE MALT: CAMPBELTOWN
46% ABV

The nose is oily, with sherry, brine, figs, and spicy peat. Citrus fruit and earthy peat on the full, oily, palate, with smoked fish and barbecue notes.

THE MACALLAN

Scotland

Easter Elchies, Craigellachie, Morayshire
www.themacallan.com

The Macallan was first licensed in 1824 as the Elchies Distillery. It was a small-scale operation: annual production was still only 40,000 gallons (180,000 liters) when it was sold to Roderick Kemp in 1892. The distillery was expanded and remained in family control until 1996, when it was bought by Highland Distillers (now part of Edrington), for $280 million. In the intervening years, the distillery was rebuilt in

◀ THE MACALLAN GOLD

SINGLE MALT: SPEYSIDE 40% ABV
The nose offers apricots and peaches, fudge, and a hint of leather. Medium-bodied, with malt, walnuts, and spices on the palate. Quite oaky in the medium-length finish.

THE MACALLAN FINE OAK 10-YEAR-OLD

SINGLE MALT: SPEYSIDE 40% ABV
With less sherry influence than the standard 10-year-old, more of the fresh, brisk, malty distillery character comes through.

the 1950s and the number of stills grew to 21. More importantly, The Macallan 10-year-old established itself as one of the leading single malts on Speyside. The distillery had always used sherry casks, which were shipped in from Spain. A deep amber color and fruitcake character came to symbolize the whisky. So the launch of the Fine Oak series in 2004, which uses bourbon casks alongside sherry butts, marked a radical departure. It has clearly widened The Macallan's appeal, however.

In 2012, The Macallan began to phase in a new core range of expressions without age statements. They are Gold, Amber, Sienna, and Ruby.

THE MACALLAN 30-YEAR-OLD ▶
SINGLE MALT: SPEYSIDE 43% ABV
A big, post-prandial malt with a sweet, sherried nose and spicy flavors of orange peel, cloves, and dates that linger on the finish.

THE MACALLAN 25-YEAR-OLD
SINGLE MALT: SPEYSIDE 43% ABV
Spicy citrus notes accompany the ripe dried-fruit character from the sherry casks, which lead to a little wood-smoke on the tongue.

MACARTHUR'S

Scotland
Owner: Inver House Distillers

The MacArthur clan of Argyllshire fought nobly alongside Robert the Bruce in the struggle for Scottish independence and subsequently gave their name to this standard blend. Like so many others, it has its roots in the upsurge of blending from independent merchants in the late-Victorian era and can be traced to the 1870s. Today it is owned by Inver House Distillers, who describe it as having a "light, smooth flavor with toffee and vanilla from cask aging." MacArthur's is not to be confused with single malts bottled independently under the label James MacArthur.

◀ **MACARTHUR'S**

BLEND 40% ABV

Fragrant, barley-malt nose with sweet, citrus aftertones. A medium-bodied, uncomplicated whisky, softly aromatic, with a smooth, mellow palate and a fresh, lingering finish.

MACKMYRA

Sweden

Mackmyra, Kolonnvägen 2, Gävle
www.mackmyra.se

Mackmyra was founded in 1999
by the Swedish engineer Magnus
Dardanell and a group of friends.
Having first released a series of six
"Preludium" expressions during
2006 and 2007, many other
bottlings have followed, and
the core range now consists of
Brukswhisky, Svensk Ek (matured
in Swedish oak barrels), and the
smoky Svensk Rök. Mackmyra
matures its spirit in several
locations, including in a series
of underground warehouses in the
old Bodås mine, 35 miles from Gävle.

MACKMYRA SVENSK EK ▶
SINGLE MALT 46.1% ABV
Toasted oak notes on the nose, with
honey and citrus fruits. More honey
and citrus notes on the palate, with
malt, ginger, pepper, and spicy oak.

MACKMYRA SVENSK RÖK
SINGLE MALT 46.1% ABV
Peat smoke, citrus fruit, and vanilla on
the nose, with a palate displaying sooty
peat, more citrus fruit, and a hint of
honey, with lingering spiciness.

MACKMYRA

SVENSK EK
SWEDISH SINGLE MALT WHISKY

Våra ekfat är tillverkade av träd som för hundratals
år sedan planterades på Visingsö för att bli virke till
Sveriges flotta. Idag ger de smak till vårt moderna
och innovativa whiskyhantverk.

| ALKOHOLHALT. | VOLYM. | MASTER |
| 46.1% VOL | 70 CL | BLENDER. |

MAKER'S MARK

US

Maker's Mark Distillery, 3350 Burks Springs Road, Loretto, Kentucky www.makersmark.com

Maker's Mark Distillery is located on the banks of Hardin's Creek, near Loretto. Established in 1805, it is the US's oldest working distillery remaining on its original site. The Maker's Mark brand was developed during the 1950s by Bill Samuels, Jr. and is now owned by Fortune Brands, Inc. The use of the Scot's spelling "whisky," rare among US brands, is a nod to Samuels' Scottish ancestry.

◀ MAKER'S MARK
BOURBON 45% ABV

A subtle, complex, and clean nose, with vanilla and spice, a delicate floral note of roses, plus lime and cocoa beans. Medium in body, it offers a palate of fresh fruit, spices, eucalyptus, and ginger cake. The finish features more spices, fresh oak with a hint of smoke, and a final flash of peach cheesecake.

240

MANNOCHMORE

Scotland
Elgin, Morayshire
www.malts.com

From its conception in 1971, Mannochmore's simple role in life was supplying malt for Haig, then the top-selling blend in the UK. Fourteen years later it fell victim to the over-supply in the industry and was mothballed, as the big distillers sought to drain the whisky loch. It was back in production by 1989 and launched its first official malt as part of the Flora & Fauna range three years later. Mannochmore is famous for launching the cult black whisky Loch Dhu in 1996.

MANNOCHMORE
FLORA & FAUNA 12-YEAR-OLD ▶
SINGLE MALT: SPEYSIDE 43% ABV
An apéritif-style malt, with a light, floral nose but, in the mouth, a more luscious, spicy character, comes through.

MANNOCHMORE RARE MALTS
22-YEAR-OLD
SINGLE MALT: SPEYSIDE 60.1% ABV
Distilled in 1974, this limited edition exudes fragrant, flowery aromas. Herbaceous and peppery, with a touch of peat in the mix.

MASTERSTROKE

India

Owner: Diageo Radico
www.radicokhaitan.com
www.diageo.com

Masterstroke De Luxe Whisky, an IMFL (Indian Made Foreign Liquor) priced for the "prestige" category, was launched by Diageo Radico in February 2007. The company is a joint 50:50 venture between Radico Khaitan, Ltd. (*see 8PM, p8*), "India's fastest-growing liquor manufacturer," and the world's largest drinks company, Diageo. It is their first joint venture. Within three months the brand was being endorsed by Bollywood superstar Shah Rukh Khan.

◀ **MASTERSTROKE**

BLEND 42.8% ABV

A rich nose and mouthfeel, lent by a liberal amount of Blair Athol single malt. Well-balanced, with the light finish characteristic of IMFLs.

MCCARTHY'S

US

Clear Creek Distillery,
2389 NW Wilson Street,
Portland, Oregon
www.clearcreekdistillery.com

Steve McCarthy established Clear
Creek Distillery in 1986, and has
been distilling whiskey for over
two decades. He is of the opinion
that, since it is made from peat-
malted barley brought in from
Scotland, "our whiskey would
be a single malt Scotch if Oregon
were Scotland."

MCCARTHY'S OREGON ▶
SINGLE MALT 40% ABV
McCarthy's is initially matured in
former sherry casks for two or three
years, then for six to twelve months
in barrels made from air-dried Oregon
oak. Kippery and spicy on the nose,
with a hint of sulfur, peat, and vanilla.
It is big-bodied and oily, smoky-sweet
on the meaty palate, and with dry oak,
malt, spice, and salt in the long finish.

243

MCCLELLAND'S

Scotland

Owner: Morrison Bowmore
www.mcclellands.co.uk

The range of McClelland's single malts offers a chance to explore Scotland and four of its key whisky-distilling regions. It was first launched in 1986, with a Highland, Lowland, and Islay expression. These proved so successful that a Speyside expression was introduced in 1999. According to the company, each one is carefully selected to

◀ MCCLELLAND'S HIGHLAND

SINGLE MALT: HIGHLANDS 40% ABV
Delicate wood notes on the nose, with sweet buttercream and fresh vanilla. Some initial sweetness, giving way to fresh fruit and lime hints.

MCCLELLAND'S ISLAY

SINGLE MALT: ISLAY 40% ABV
The nose is unmistakably Islay: wood smoke and cinders, tar, vanilla, and citrus hints. Forceful sea salt, burned oak, and peat smoke, with vanilla undertones on the palate.

reflect the true essence and character of the region in which it is produced.

The brand currently claims to be number four in the US market, where it competes against the likes of Glenlivet, Glenfiddich, and The Macallan. McClelland's is also distributed to global markets, including Austria, South Africa, Japan, Canada, France, Russia, and the Netherlands.

MCCLELLAND'S LOWLAND ▶
SINGLE MALT: LOWLANDS 40% ABV
A richly floral nose with hints of nutmeg, ginger, and citrus fruits. Very clean and delicate on the palate, with floral notes.

MCCLELLAND'S SPEYSIDE
SINGLE MALT: SPEYSIDE 40% ABV
Fresh mint, cut pine, hints of dark chocolate, and sweet malt on the nose. Initially sweet, developing nutty flavors and floral hints.

MCDOWELL'S

India

Owner: United Spirits
www.unitedspirits.in

Scotsman Angus McDowell founded McDowell & Co. in Madras in 1826 as a trading company specializing in liquor and cigars. McDowell's No.1 was launched in 1968.

A malt whisky distillery was commissioned by McDowell & Co. at Ponda, Goa, in 1971. The spirit is matured in ex-bourbon casks for around three years. It is claimed that the heat and humidity of Goa leads to a more rapid maturation.

The product is described as "the first-ever indigenously developed single malt whisky in Asia."

◀ MCDOWELL'S NO.1 RESERVE

BLEND 42.8% ABV

"Blended with Scotch and Select Indian Malts," this has a nose of dried figs and sweet tobacco and, later, prunes and dates. A sweet taste initially, then burned sugar and a short finish.

MCDOWELL'S SINGLE MALT

SINGLE MALT 42.8% ABV

With fresh cereal and fruit on the nose and a sweet, pleasantly citric taste, this is not unlike a young Speyside.

MELLOW CORN

US

Heaven Hill Distillery,
1701 West Breckinridge Street,
Louisville, Kentucky
www.heavenhill.com

According to Heaven Hill, "The forerunner and kissing cousin to Bourbon, American straight corn whiskey is defined by the US Government as having a recipe or mashbill with a minimum of 81 percent corn, the rest being malted barley and rye."

Today, Heaven Hill is the sole remaining national producer of this classic whiskey style, bottling Georgia Moon (*see p126*) in addition to Mellow Corn.

MELLOW CORN ▶

CORN WHISKEY 50% ABV

Wood varnish and vanilla, with floral and herbal notes on the nose. The palate is big, oily, and fruity, with candy apples. More fruit, toffee, and understated vanilla complete the finish. Young and boisterous.

MICHAEL COLLINS

Ireland
Owner: Beam Suntory

Despite the fame of General Michael Collins among the Irish people, most of them have never heard of this whiskey. It was initially formulated for the American market by Cooley Distillery in conjunction with US importer Sidney Frank. However, it can now be bought on both sides of the Atlantic.

Unusually for an Irish whiskey, the malt is double-distilled and has a light peating, too. The blend is a mix of the malt and a younger grain whiskey, matured in bourbon casks.

◀ MICHAEL COLLINS SINGLE MALT

SINGLE MALT 40% ABV
Soft and drinkable, with plenty of cookie flavors. Vanilla notes emerge, with a hint of light smoke.

MICHAEL COLLINS BLEND

BLEND 40% ABV
Less impressive than the malt. It is thin, with the scent of woody embers at its core, but it lacks a decent finish.

MICHTER'S

US

Michter's Distillery,
2351 New Millennium Drive,
Louisville, Kentucky
www.michters.com

Michter's whiskey was distilled in Pennsylvania until 1989, when its owners were declared bankrupt and the distillery closed down. The brand name was resurrected by businessmen Joseph J. Magliocco and Dick Newman a few years later, and production now takes place in the Michter's Distillery in the Shively section of Louisville, Kentucky. A number of ryes and bourbons are marketed under the Michter's label, along with an unblended American whiskey and a sour mash whiskey.

MICHTER'S US NO.1 BOURBON ▶

BOURBON 45.7% ABV
Very spicy on the nose, with caramel, apricots, and cinnamon. Sweet palate delivery, with more apricots, cloves, black pepper, and a smoky note. Spicy oak in the finish.

MIDLETON

Ireland
Midleton, County Cork
www.irishdistillers.ie

Among all the spirits produced at Midleton—Jameson, Powers, Paddy, and all of the Irish Distillers' portfolio of whiskeys—there is just one regularly appearing whiskey that carries the actual Midleton moniker. Launched in 1984, Midleton Very Rare is for the premium market and the price reflects whatever that market can bear. A new vintage is released late every year, with little variation.

◀ MIDLETON VERY RARE
BLEND 40% ABV
On the nose, classy oak and bold cereal notes dance on a high wire made of pure beeswax. The body is full and yielding, and the finish breaks on the tongue in waves of silky, walnut whip.

MIDLETON MASTER DISTILLER'S PRIVATE COLLECTION 1973
PURE POT STILL 56% ABV
A bottling of pure pot still whiskey from the old Midleton Distillery. Just 800 bottles were released. Its taste is said to be spicy, fruity, and honeyed, with some dry, sherry nuttiness.

MILFORD

New Zealand

*The New Zealand Malt Whisky
Company & Preston Associates,
14–16 Harbour St., Oamaru
www.thenzwhisky.com*

Milford whisky was originally
made at Willowbank Distillery
in Dunedin, South Island, which
was owned by the Wilson Brewery
(*see Lammerlaw, p220*). The New
Zealand Malt Whisky Company
now owns the Milford label (and
also the less prestigious Prestons
label). It has opened a retail
warehouse named Cellar Door at
Oamaru, where a wide range of
expressions of New Zealand
whisky are available.

MILFORD 10-YEAR-OLD ▶

SINGLE MALT 43% ABV
Often compared to a Scottish Lowland
malt, Milford's 10-year-old has a light,
dry, and fragrant nose; the taste is
sweet, then dry, with a slightly
woody, short finish.

MILLSTONE

The Netherlands

*Zuidam, Weverstraat 6, 5111 PW,
Baarle Nassau*
www.zuidam-distillers.com

What started as a gin distillery
some 50 years ago is now a
company with a second generation
of the Zuidam family at the helm.
It produces beautifully crafted
single malts, alongside excellent
young and old jenevers, as the
Dutch call their gin. The Millstone
5-year-old single malt whisky was
introduced in 2007, to be followed
by an 8-year-old sibling. Zuidam
uses ex-bourbon as well as
ex-sherry casks to mature its
whisky. A 10-year-old expression
is in the making.

◀ MILLSTONE 5-YEAR-OLD

SINGLE MALT 40% ABV
Delicate aromas of fruit and honey
combined with vanilla, wood, and a
hint of coconut. Rich honey sweetness
in the mouth, delicate spicy notes, and
a long vanilla-oak finish.

MILTONDUFF

Scotland
Miltonduff, Elgin, Morayshire

Miltonduff was one of supposedly more than 50 illicit stills in Elgin until it took out a licence in 1824. In 1936, it was bought by George Ballantine & Son. From 1964 until 1981, the distillery had a pair of Lomond stills, allowing it to produce different styles of whisky, such as the single malt Mosstowie. These are now increasingly rare. Pernod Ricard bought Miltonduff in 2005, and uses much of the 1.3 million-gallon (5.8 million-liter) production to supply malt for its Ballantine's Finest blend. An official 16-year-old cask strength malt is now available, with several more bottlings existing among independents.

MILTONDUFF 16-YEAR-OLD ▶
SINGLE MALT: SPEYSIDE 52.9% ABV
Soft nose, with vanilla and citrus, continuing through the cinnamon and toffee palate. Lengthy finish.

MONKEY SHOULDER

Scotland
Owner: William Grant & Sons

The name may seem contrived, but this blended malt from William Grant & Sons refers to a condition known among workers in the maltings—turning the damp grain by hand, they often incurred a repetitive strain injury.

Three metal monkeys decorate the shoulder of the bottle and just three single malts go into the blend—Glenfiddich, Balvenie, and Kininvie. At the launch, great play was made of the whisky's mixability, and you're as likely to encounter it on a cocktail menu as you are in your local liquor store.

◀ MONKEY SHOULDER
BLEND 40% ABV

Banana, honey, pears, and allspice on the nose. Vanilla, nutmeg, citrus hints, and generic fruit on the palate. A dry finish, then a short burst of menthol.

MORTLACH

Scotland
Dufftown, Keith, Banffshire
www.mortlach.com

The six stills at Mortlach are configured in a complex manner, with a fifth of the spirit being triple-distilled in an intermediate still called "Wee Witchie." This process is intended to add richness and depth to the spirit, which is then condensed in traditional worm tubs outdoors, to create a more robust style of whisky.

Mortlach is ever-popular with blenders, but 2014 saw the single malt given a greatly enhanced profile, with the release of four new expressions.

MORTLACH RARE OLD ▶
SINGLE MALT: SPEYSIDE 43.4% ABV
Fresh on the nose; with peaches and apricots, milk chocolate, and caramel. Fruit carries over from the nose to the nutty palate, with cinnamon spice.

MORTLACH 25-YEAR-OLD
SINGLE MALT: SPEYSIDE 43.4% ABV
A hint of fresh soil on the nose, with apples, and a slight meatiness. Malt, muted spices, and interplay between sweet and savory on the palate.

MURREE

Pakistan

Murree Distillery, National Park Road, Rawalpindi
www.murreebrewery.com

With a dispensation having been granted to the non-Muslim owners of Murree to distill alcoholic drinks "for visitors and non-Muslims," this is the only distillery of alcoholic beverages in a Muslim country.

The barley comes from the UK and is malted in floor maltings and Saladin boxes. Some of the spirit is filled into cask, most into large vats (some made from Australian oak), and matured in cellars equipped with a cooling system.

◀ MURREE'S CLASSIC 8-YEAR-OLD

SINGLE MALT 43% ABV
A flowery nose and finish, somewhat green, with a hard candy taste. Unlikely to be pure malt whisky.

MURREE'S RAREST 21-YEAR-OLD

SINGLE MALT 43% ABV
This is the oldest whisky to have been produced in Asia. The Murree key notes have developed and deepened with a big dose of wood-extractive flavors.

NANT

Australia
The Nant Estate, Bothwell, Tasmania
www.nant.com.au

The Nant estate in Tasmania, founded in 1821, was bought by Keith and Margaret Batt in 2004 with a view to building a distillery on the historic working farm. With the expert guidance of Bill Lark (*see p224*), the distillery went into production in April 2008. The plan is to produce a limited number of casks each year. The barley and water for the distillery come from the estate, while a restored mill provides the grist. There is also an elegant new visitor center.

(see p224)

NANT DOUBLE MALT ▶
BLENDED MALT 43% ABV
This is a vatting of two casks selected from other Tasmanian distilleries, and gives an idea of what Nant's own whisky will taste like. Sweet and fruity, with plums and cream soda, it is medium-bodied and smooth.

NIKKA—GRAIN & BLENDS

Japan

Nikka 1, Aobaku, Sendaishi, Miyagiken; Kurokawacho 7–6, Yoichimachi, Yoichigun, Hokkaido www.nikka.com

Japan's second-largest distillery company was founded in 1933 by Masataka Taketsuru. This charismatic distiller had learned the art of whisky-making in Scotland—at Longmorn in Speyside and Hazelburn in Campbeltown. He then went

◀ NIKKA WHISKY FROM THE BARREL

BLEND 51.4% ABV

The nose is upfront and slightly floral, with good intensity, peachiness, and a lift akin to rosemary oil and pine sap. The palate is lightly sweet, with some vanilla, a hint of cherry, and plenty of spiciness on the finish. This is a top blend.

NIKKA ALL MALT

BLENDED MALT 40% ABV

A blend of pot still malt and 100 percent malt from a Coffey still. Sweet and dry oak on the nose alongside some banana. The palate is soft and unctuous.

to Hokkaido island in Japan, where conditions were closer to those in Scotland, and founded Yoichi distillery. His company, Nikka, operates two malt distilleries at Yoichi and Miyagikyo. It also has grain plants and a growing portfolio of styles including blends and single malts.

In recent years, Nikka has been focusing on the export market. Although its blends are available overseas, its commercial push has been through its single-malt range branded as Nikka Miyagikyo (*see* *p260*) and Nikka Yoichi (*p262*).

NIKKA PURE MALT RED ▶

BLENDED MALT 43% ABV
Nikka produces a blended malt range called the Pure Malt Series. The Red is light and fragrant, with faint hints of pineapple, fresh apple, pear, and a gentle almondlike oakiness.

NIKKA COFFEY MALT WHISKY

MALT WHISKY 45% ABV
Lemon sprinkled with black pepper and background vanilla on the feisty nose. The palate continues those themes, with the addition of milky coffee and prune juice.

NIKKA MIYAGIKYO

Japan
Nikka 1, Aobaku, Sendaishi, Miyagiken
www.nikka.com

Also known as Sendai after its nearest town, Miyagikyo was the second distillery built by Nikka. Today, it has a malt distillery with eight stills, a grain plant with two different set-ups, and extensive warehousing. The predominant style is lightly fragrant and softly fruity, but there are some peaty examples, too.

◄ NIKKA MIYAGIKYO 10-YEAR-OLD
SINGLE MALT 45% ABV
Typical of the main distillery character, this has an attractive floral lift (lilies, hot gorse, lilac), with a touch of anise in the background. The palate shows balanced, crisp oak, some butterscotch notes, and a pinelike finish.

NIKKA MIYAGIKYO
SINGLE MALT 45% ABV
The extra two years fill out the nose with flowers, giving way to soft tropical fruits, such as mango and persimmon, as well as a richer vanilla pod character. Good structure, with a wisp of smoke.

NIKKA TAKETSURU

Japan
*Nikka 1, Aobaku, Sendaishi,
Miyagiken; Kurokawacho 7–6,
Yoichimachi, Yoichigun, Hokkaido*
www.nikka.com

This small range of blended
(vatted) malts is named after
the founder of Nikka, Masataka
Taketsuru. Like the Pure Malt
Series, it is made up of
component whiskies from
the firm's two sites.

NIKKA TAKETSURU
17-YEAR-OLD ▶
BLENDED MALT 43% ABV
There's obvious smoke at work here:
some cigar-box aromas, varnish, and
light leather. When diluted, a fresh
tropical-fruit character comes out.
This is what leads on the palate, before
the peat smoke begins to assert itself.

NIKKA TAKETSURU
21-YEAR-OLD
BLENDED MALT 43% ABV
With this multi-award winner, the
smoke is immediate while the spirit
behind is thicker, richer, and darker:
ripe berries, cake mix, oak, and
a touch of mushroom or truffle
indicative of age. Fruit syrups,
figs, prunes, and smoke.

NIKKA YOICHI

Japan
Kurokawacho 7–6, Yoichimachi,
Yoichigun, Hokkaido
www.nikka.com

Although Yoichi's malts are most definitely Japanese, they do have close resemblances to their cousins in Scotland—the whiskies of Islay and Campbeltown in particular. A wide range of styles is made, but Yoichi is famous for its complex, robust, oily, and smoky malts.

◀ NIKKA YOICHI 10-YEAR-OLD
SINGLE MALT 45% ABV
There's a hint of maltiness in here. Salt spray and light smoke on the nose initially, with some caramelized fruit notes. Yoichi's oiliness coats the tongue while the smoke changes from fragrant to sooty with dried flowers in the finish.

NIKKA YOICHI 12-YEAR-OLD
SINGLE MALT 45% ABV
This is classic Yoichi—big, deep, robust, and complex. The peatiness adds an earthy character to the coal-like sootiness. Poached pear and baked peach give a balancing sweetness, offset by smoke, licorice, and heather.

THE NOTCH

US

Triple Eight Distillery,
5&7 Bartlett Farm Road,
Nantucket, Massachusetts
www.ciscobrewers.com

Dean and Melissa Long started up
their Nantucket Winery in 1981,
and added the Cisco Brewery
in 1995. Two years later they
founded the region's first micro-
distillery, Triple Eight. The first
single malt whiskey was distilled
in 2000 and is called The Notch
Whisky, because it is "not Scotch,"
though it is produced in the
Scottish style. It is matured
in former bourbon barrels before
being finished in French oak
Merlot barrels.

THE NOTCH ▶

SINGLE MALT 44.4% ABV

Sweet aromas of almonds and fruit on
the nose, backed by vanilla and toasted
oak. Mellow honey and pear notes are
present on the palate, which also
contains a suggestion of Merlot.
The finish is lengthy and herbal.

OBAN

Scotland
Oban, Argyll
www.malts.com

Oban Distillery dates back to 1793, when Oban itself was a tiny fishing village. The town (dubbed "Gateway to the Isles") now surrounds the distillery and prevents any expansion. Due to its small capacity of 150,000 gallons (700,000 liters), Oban was never closed during periods of overproduction, and so it has been in almost continuous production since it was built. Alongside the official no-age Little Bay and 14-year-old statements, double-matured Distillers Edition malts are released from time to time.

◀ OBAN 14-YEAR-OLD
SINGLE MALT: HIGHLANDS 43% ABV
The brisk, maritime distillery character is mellowed by the years in wood. It has a rich, dried-fruit character.

OBAN DISTILLERS EDITION 1992
SINGLE MALT: HIGHLANDS 43% ABV
A 15-year-old malt, aged in different casks during maturation. Spicy and oaky flavors dominate from the strong sherry-wood effect.

OFFICER'S CHOICE

India
Owner: Allied Blenders and Distillers
www.abdindia.com

Available in some 18 countries, Officer's Choice has become one of the largest whiskey brands in the world since its 1988 launch. Sales have risen at 14 percent per annum over the past five years, with sales of 23 million cases between 2014 and 2015. It enjoys a 37 percent share in the Indian whisky market, jostling for a top spot with McDowell's No.1 Reserve. Two "semi-premium" variants of Officer's Choice are also available: Blue, which appeared in 2012, and Black, released two years later. All expressions comprise Indian grain whisky and Scottish blended malts.

OFFICER'S CHOICE ▶
BLEND 42.8% ABV
The nose is spirity, with a hint of rum, while the palate yields caramel and cinnamon before a short finish.

OLD CHARTER

US

Buffalo Trace Distillery,
1001 Wilkinson Boulevard,
Frankfort, Kentucky
www.buffalotracedistillery.com

The Old Charter brand dates back to 1874, and the name is a direct reference to the Charter Oak tree, where Connecticut's colonial charter was hidden from the English in 1687. The Buffalo Trace Distillery itself dates back to the early 1900s and is listed on the National Register of Historic Places.

◀ OLD CHARTER 8-YEAR-OLD

BOURBON 40% ABV

Initially dry and peppery on the nose, with sweet and buttery aromas following through. Mouth-coating, with fruit, vanilla, old leather, and cloves on the palate. The finish is long and sophisticated.

OLD CROW

US

*Jim Beam Distillery,
149 Happy Hollow Road,
Clermont, Kentucky
www.beamsuntory.com*

Old Crow takes its name from the 19th-century Scottish-born chemist and Kentucky distiller James Christopher Crow. Along with Old Grand-Dad (*see p270*) and Old Taylor (*see p275*), this brand was acquired by Jim Beam from National Distillers in 1987, and the three distilleries associated with these bourbons were closed. All production now takes place at Jim Beam's distilleries in Boston and Clermont.

OLD CROW ▶

BOURBON 40% ABV

Complex on the nose, with malt, rye, and sharp fruit notes combining with gentle spice. The palate follows through with spicy, malty, and citric elements, with citrus and spice notes to the fore.

OLD FITZGERALD

US

Heaven Hill Distillery,
1701 West Breckinridge Street,
Louisville, Kentucky
www.heavenhill.com

Old Fitzgerald was named by John E. Fitzgerald, who founded a distillery at Frankfort in 1870. The brand moved to its present home of Louisville when the Stitzel brothers, Frederick and Philip, merged their company with that of William Larue Weller & Sons, and subsequently opened the new Stitzel-Weller distillery at Louisville in 1935.

◄ VERY SPECIAL OLD FITZGERALD 12-YEAR-OLD

BOURBON 45% ABV

A complex and well-balanced bourbon, made with some wheat in the mashbill, rather than rye. The nose is rich, fruity, and leathery, while the palate exhibits sweet and fruity notes balanced by spices and oak. The finish is long and drying, with vanilla fading to oak.

OLD FORESTER

US

Brown-Forman Distillery,
850 Dixie Highway,
Louisville, Kentucky
www.oldforester.com

The origins of the Old Forester brand date back to 1870, when George Garvin Brown established a distillery in Louisville, Kentucky. The whiskey initially used the spelling "Forrester," and some say the name was selected to honor Confederate army officer General Nathan Bedford Forrest.

OLD FORESTER ▶

BOURBON 43% ABV

Complex, with pronounced floral notes, vanilla, spice, pepper, fruit, chocolate, and menthol on the nose. Full and fruity in the mouth, where rye and peaches vie with fudge, nutmeg, and oak. The finish offers more rye, toffee, licorice, and drying oak.

OLD FORESTER BIRTHDAY BOURBON (2007)

BOURBON 47% ABV

The 2007 release is sweet on the nose, with cinnamon, caramel, vanilla, and mint. The palate is full and complex, with caramel, apples, and vanilla oak. The finish is lengthy, warm, and clean.

OLD GRAND-DAD

US

Jim Beam Distillery,
149 Happy Hollow Road,
Clermont, Kentucky
www.beamsuntory.com

Old Grand-Dad was established in 1882 by a grandson of distiller Basil Hayden (*see p38*). The brand and its distillery eventually passed into the hands of American Brands (now Fortune Brands Inc.) which subsequently closed the distillery. Production now takes place in the Jim Beam distilleries in Clermont and Boston.

◀ **OLD GRAND-DAD**

BOURBON 43–57% ABV

Made with a comparatively high percentage of rye, the nose of Old Grand-Dad reveals oranges and peppery spices. Quite heavy-bodied, the taste is full, yet surprisingly smooth, considering the strength. Fruit, nuts, and caramel are foremost on the palate, while the finish is long and oily.

OLD PARR

Scotland
Owner: Diageo

The original "Old Parr" was one Thomas Parr, who lived from 1483 to 1635, making him 152 years old when he died. If that seems improbable, his tomb can be inspected in Poets' Corner, Westminster Abbey.

In 1871, Old Parr's name was borrowed by two famous blenders of their day, the Greenlees brothers, for their deluxe whisky. Now under the stewardship of industry giants Diageo, the brand has gone on to success in Japan, Venezuela, Mexico, and Colombia. By tradition, Cragganmore is the mainstay of the blend.

GRAND OLD PARR 12-YEAR-OLD ▶
BLEND 43% ABV

Pronounced malt, raisin, and orange notes on the nose, with some apple and dried-fruit undertones, and perhaps a hint of peat. Forceful on the palate, with flavors of malt, raisin, burned caramel, and brown sugar.

OLD POTRERO

US

Anchor Distilling Company,
1705 Marisposa Street,
San Francisco, California
www.anchorbrewing.com

Fritz Maytag is one of the pioneers of the American "micro-drinks" movement. In 1994 he added a small distillery to his brewery on San Francisco's Potrero Hill. Here, Maytag aims to "re-create the original whiskey of America," by making small batches of spirits in traditional, open pot stills, using 100 percent rye malt.

◀ OLD POTRERO 18TH CENTURY STYLE WHISKEY

SINGLE MALT RYE 62.55% ABV

An award-winning, "18th century style" whiskey distilled in a small pot still, then aged for a year in new, lightly toasted oak barrels. Floral, nutty nose, with vanilla and spice. Smooth on the palate, with mint, honey, and pepper in the lengthy finish.

OLD PULTENEY

Scotland

Pulteney Distillery, Wick, Caithness
www.oldpulteney.com

Wick was a tiny village when the British Fisheries Society, under the directorship of Sir William Pulteney decided to turn it into a model fishing port in the 1790s. In 1826, with the trade in herring booming, local distiller James Henderson named his new distillery in his honor.

The solitary wash still comes with a giant ball, to increase reflux, and a truncated top, supposedly lopped off to fit the still room.

OLD PULTENEY 12-YEAR-OLD ▶

SINGLE MALT: HIGHLANDS 40% ABV
A brisk, salty, maritime malt with a woody sweetness from aging in bourbon casks.

OLD PULTENEY 17-YEAR-OLD

SINGLE MALT: HIGHLANDS 46% ABV
The 17-year-old is partly matured in sherry wood, to add fruity, butterscotch notes to the flavor. Medium-full body in the mouth, with a long finish.

OLD SMUGGLER

Scotland
Owner: Gruppo Campari

Reputedly, and appropriately, a big favorite during Prohibition, Old Smuggler was first developed by James and George Stodart in 1835. Although the firm is today largely forgotten, history records that it was the first to marry its whisky in sherry butts. The brand is now owned by Gruppo Campari, who acquired it along with its sister blend Braemar and the flagship Glen Grant Distillery from Pernod Ricard in 2006. It continues to hold a significant position in the US and Argentina, where it is the second-bestselling whisky, and is reported to be developing strong sales in Eastern Europe.

◀ **OLD SMUGGLER**
BLEND 40% ABV
Decent Scotch with no offensive overtones and some smoke hints. Blended for value, and for drinking with a mixer.

OLD TAYLOR

US

Jim Beam Distillery,
149 Happy Hollow Road,
Clermont, Kentucky

Old Taylor was introduced by
Edmund Haynes Taylor, Jr., who
was associated at various times
with three distilleries in the
Frankfort area of Kentucky,
including what is now Buffalo
Trace (*see p66*). He was the
man responsible for the Bottled-
in-Bond Act of 1897, which
guaranteed a whiskey's quality—
any bottle bearing an official
government seal had to be 100
proof (50% ABV) and at least four
years old. Old Taylor was bought
by Fortune Brands in 1987.

OLD TAYLOR ▶

BOURBON 40% ABV

Light and orangey on the nose, with
a hint of marzipan; sweet, honeyed,
and slightly oaky on the palate.

275

OVEREEM

Australia
*Old Hobart Distillery,
Blackman's Bay, Tasmania*
www.overeem.co.uk

Businessman Casey Overeem visited no fewer than 15 distilleries in one trip to the UK to expand his knowledge of the distillation process. He returned to his native Tasmania to build the Old Hobart distillery and began whisky production there in 2007.

Distillation takes place in a pair of copper pot stills, using a lightly peated wash from the nearby Lark Distillery. The whisky is matured in ex-bourbon, port, or sherry casks.

In 2014, the Lark Distillery bought the Old Hobart distillery along with the Overeem brand.

◄ OVEREEM PORT MATURED—CASK STRENGTH

SINGLE MALT 60% ABV
Summer fruits and vanilla on the softly spicy nose, while the palate offers more vanilla and spice.

OVEREEM BOURBON CASK MATURED—CASK STRENGTH

SINGLE MALT 60% ABV
Nutty vanilla and caramel on the nose. Big flavors of ripe apple and coconut.

P&M

France
Domaine Mavela, Brasserie Pietra,
Route de La Marana, 20600 Furiani,
Corsica
www.brasseriepietra.com

P&M is a fruitful cooperation
between two companies on the
Mediterranean island of Corsica.
Founded as a brewery in 1996,
Pietra produces the mash that is
distilled at Mavela. The pure malt
whisky is aged in casks made of
oak from the local forest. Other
spirits produced at Mavela include
P&M Blend and P&M Blend
Supérieur. Cask type and age
are not specified.

P&M PURE MALT ▶
MALT 42% ABV
This complex, aromatic whisky
has a subtle aroma of honey, apricot,
and citrus fruit, and a rich flavor.

PADDY

Ireland
*Midleton Distillery,
Midleton, County Cork
www.irishdistillers.ie*

There was a time when Irish
whiskey was sold anonymously
from casks in pubs. What whiskey
a pub stocked was down to the
owner and his relationship with
the agent for the distillery.

Paddy Flaherty was an agent
for the Cork Distilleries Company
of Midleton in the 1920s and '30s.
You knew when he was in town,
because he'd buy everyone drinks
at the bar, and the whiskey he
sold—the CDC's Old Irish
Whiskey—became so synonymous
with the man himself that it was
simply known as Paddy's whiskey.

◀ PADDY
BLEND 40% ABV
This is a malty dram, which is both
solid and well matured. It offers
a satisfying, spicy, peppery kick.

PASSPORT

Scotland
Owner: Chivas Brothers

Passport was developed by Seagram and acquired by Pernod Ricard in 2002. Passport's main strongholds are the US, South Korea, Spain, and Brazil, where its fruity taste lends itself to being served on the rocks, in mixed drinks, and in cocktails. Packaged in a distinctive retro, rectangular green bottle, Passport is "a unique Scotch whisky, inspired by the revolution of 1960s Britain, with a young and vibrant personality." Such distinguished and famous malts as Glenlivet are found in the blend.

PASSPORT ▶

BLEND 40% ABV

A fruity taste and a deliciously creamy finish. It can be served straight or, more usually, mixed over ice. Medium-bodied, with a soft and mellow finish.

PAUL JOHN

India

*John Distilleries Pvt. Ltd.,
110, Pantharapalya, Mysore Road,
Bangalore 560 039
www.pauljohnwhisky.com*

Paul John single malts are produced on the tropical coast of Goa, using six-row barley grown on the foothills of the Himalayas. Distillation takes place in traditional copper pot stills, which can yield up to 660 gallons (3,000 liters) of spirit per day. Casks are stored in a temperature-controlled cellar, but the climate of Goa means that whiskeys mature relatively quickly. The first single malt was distilled in 2007 and the initial release took place in autumn 2012.

◄ PAUL JOHN EDITED
SINGLE MALT 46% ABV
The nose is fruity, with coffee and gentle smoke. Grassy and peaty on the palate, with more coffee coming through.

PAUL JOHN BRILLIANCE
SINGLE MALT 46% ABV
Honey, cinnamon, and spice on the fragrant nose. Sweet, spicy, and smooth on the palate, with a suggestion of milk chocolate.

PENDERYN

Wales

Penderyn, near Aberdare
www.welsh-whisky.co.uk

Whisky-making in Wales has ancient roots: according to Penderyn, the Welsh may have been producing *"gwirod"* in the 4th century. The industry fell silent during the 20th century until Penderyn was established in 2004, the first Welsh microdistillery in almost 100 years. HRH Prince Charles opened its doors to the public in June 2008, eight years after the first distillate ran off the single still. The core range today includes Legend, Peated, and Myth, with the latter undergoing its entire maturation in ex-bourbon casks.

PENDERYN LEGEND ▶
SINGLE MALT 41% ABV
Light on the nose with tropical fruit, while the palate yields vanilla, honey, and fruit, notably ripe bananas, leading into a relatively short peppery finish.

PENDERYN PEATED
SINGLE MALT 46% ABV
Aromatic smoke followed by vanilla, green apples, and refreshing citrus notes.

PIG'S NOSE

Scotland
Owner: Spencerfield Spirits
www.spencerfieldspirit.com

Should you visit one of the UK's many agricultural or county fairs, you may well encounter this whisky being sold from the back of an old horse box. Do not walk away: Pig's Nose has been re-blended by Whyte & Mackay's superstar master blender, Richard Paterson, and launched back on to the market in smart new livery. Brother to the better-known blended malt Sheep Dip (*see p312*), Pig's Nose is a full-flavored and drinkable blend that more than lives up to the claim that "our Scotch is as soft and smooth as a pig's nose."

◀ PIG'S NOSE
BLEND 40% ABV
The nose is delicate and refined, with soft and sensual floral notes supported by complex fruit flavors. On the palate, there is a forceful array of malty flavors from Scotland's four distilling regions.

PIKESVILLE

US
*Heaven Hill Distillery,
1701 West Breckinridge Street,
Louisville, Kentucky*
www.pikesvillerye.com

Rye whiskeys fall into two stylistic types, namely the spicy, tangy Pennsylvania style, as exemplified by Rittenhouse (*see* *p296*), and the Maryland style, which is softer in character. Pikesville is arguably the only example of Maryland rye still being produced today. This whiskey takes its name from Pikesville in Maryland, where it was first distilled during the 1890s and last produced in 1972. A decade later the brand was acquired by Heaven Hill.

PIKESVILLE SUPREME ▶
RYE WHISKEY 40% ABV
The crisp nose presents bubble gum, fruit, and wood varnish, while on the palate there is more bubble gum, spice, oak, and overt vanilla. The finish comprises lingering vanilla and oranges.

PINWINNIE ROYALE

Scotland
Owner: Inver House Distillers

Pinwinnie Royale stands out from the crowd, its label hinting at an early ecclesiastical manuscript and regal connections, though there is little to support these romantic suppositions. Given its place in the Inver House stable, it would seem likely that Old Pulteney, Speyburn, anCnoc, and Balblair single malts are to be found in the blend, with the emphasis on the lesser-known names. As well as the standard expression, there is a 12-year-old version which mixes a light Speyside fruitiness with drier background wood notes, and a buttery texture.

◀ PINWINNIE ROYALE
BLEND 40% ABV
Young, spirity fruitiness on the nose, smooth-textured but spicy in the mouth, with burned, sooty notes in the finish.

THE POGUES

Ireland

*West Cork Distillers, Market Street,
Skibbereen, County Cork*
www.thepoguesirishwhiskey.com

The official Irish whiskey
of legendary band The Pogues,
this blend is produced by West
Cork Distillers in Skibereen.
It was launched during 2015,
and, according to the whiskey's
promoters, it is "sunlight and
barley held together with water
and left in an oak barrel for three
years and a day. This whiskey
is a measure of who we are,
made with the sole intention of
spreading that same raucous joy."

THE POGUES ▶
BLEND 40% ABV
The nose is floral and nutty, with
almonds and malt. Sweet, smooth,
and malty on the palate, with milk
chocolate, spice, and citrus fruit.

POIT DHUBH

Scotland
Owner: The Gaelic Whisky Co.
www.gaelicwhisky.com

Pràban na Linne (known also as the Gaelic Whisky Co.) was established by Sir Iain Noble in 1976 to create employment in the south of Skye. The business has grown steadily since. Poit Dhubh (pronounced *Potch Ghoo*) is a non–chill filtered blended malt supplied as 8-, 12-, and 21-year-olds.

A limited-edition 30-year-old was bottled for the company's 30th anniversary. Poit Dhubh makes much play of the possible bootleg nature of its whisky, stating, "We are unwilling either to confirm or deny that Poit Dhubh comes from an illicit still." This is, of course, complete fantasy.

◀ POIT DHUBH 8-YEAR-OLD
BLENDED MALT 43% ABV
Dried fruits and a light spiciness give a bittersweet character, with dry, woody notes and a trace of peat.

PORT ELLEN

Scotland
Port Ellen, Isle of Islay

Of all Islay malts, Port Ellen has possibly the largest cult following, owing to its rarity, which has increased every year since the distillery shut down in 1983. It was founded in 1825 by Alexander Kerr Mackay, and remained in family hands until the 1920s, when it became part of DCL (Distillers Company Ltd.). Its misfortune was to be part of the same stable as Lagavulin and Caol Ila: when the downturn came, it was the weakest link. Today it remains active as a maltings plant, supplying Islay's distilleries with most of their malt.

PORT ELLEN DOUGLAS LAING 26-YEAR-OLD ▶

SINGLE MALT: ISLAY 50% ABV
Matured in refill bourbon casks, this bottling has a sweet and fruity nose, with some new leather. Sweetness on the palate, but overwhelmed by peat smoke. A long, tarry finish, with a dab of salt.

POWERS

Ireland

*Midleton Distillery,
Midleton, County Cork
www.irishdistillers.ie*

For longer than anyone could
remember, Jameson and Powers
used to stare each other down
across the River Liffey in the
heart of Dublin. The Powers
family (on Dublin's south side)
had been in the business since
1817, and a member of the family
sat on the board of Irish Distillers
until it was incorporated into the
Pernod Ricard group, some 171
years later.

◀ POWERS GOLD LABEL

BLEND 40% ABV

This whiskey is something really
special. The nose is classically Irish—
at once bracing and brittle. At core,
this whiskey is pure pot still, cut with
just enough good grain. Powers Gold
Label is an utterly captivating blend.

POWERS GOLD LABEL
12-YEAR-OLD

BLEND 40% ABV

An older, more layered expression of
the same Powers formulation. Spice,
honey, crème brûlée, with soft wood
tones and sweet, fresh fruits.

PRIME BLUE

Scotland
Owner: Morrison Bowmore

Prime Blue is a blended malt
available largely in South East
Asia. The color blue is said to
convey nobility and royalty, and
the brand name was reputedly
chosen to reflect sophistication
in the whisky's taste. At their
peak, sales exceeded 1 million
cases a year, although the market
for this style in the Far East
has declined somewhat in
recent years and competition
from other brands has intensified.

PRIME BLUE ▶
BLENDED MALT 40% ABV
Aromas of vanilla and malted barley
are soon followed by light cocoa, and
then heathery, floral notes. Initially
fruity on the palate, followed by a
malty sweetness, and a long finish.

QUEEN ANNE

Scotland
Owner: Chivas Brothers

A good example of an "orphan brand" that has found its way into the portfolio of a larger company and appears to lack any clear role and purpose, Queen Anne was once a leading name from the distinguished Edinburgh blenders Hill, Thomson & Co. It was first produced in 1884 and blended by one William Shaw. Today it belongs to Chivas Brothers. Like so many once-famous and proud brands, Queen Anne has been left bereft and isolated by consolidation in the Scotch whisky industry, steadfastly clinging on in one or more regions where once it was loved and popular.

◀ **QUEEN ANNE**
BLEND 40% ABV
Not especially characterful, as the flavors are so tightly integrated that it is difficult to discern individual aromas or tastes. A standard blend for mixing.

RAGTIME

US

New York Distilling Company,
Richardson Street, Brooklyn, New York
www.nydistilling.com

Although the first distilleries
in Brooklyn, New York, were
established in the 18th century,
there was no legal whiskey
distillation in the "Big Apple" after
Prohibition. That was until 2009
when Tom Potter, cofounder of
Brooklyn Brewery, and Allen Katz,
former chairman of Slow Food
USA, established the New York
Distilling Co. In 2015, it started
retailing its Ragtime Rye alongside
its range of gins. This straight rye
has a mashbill of 72 percent
rye, 16 percent corn, and 12
percent barley, and has been aged
for three years and six months.

RAGTIME RYE ▶
RYE WHISKEY 45.2% ABV
Rye spice, oak, and red berries on the
nose. The palate is full, with peppery
rye, cinnamon, nutmeg, and caramel.
Finally drying, with licorice, spice,
and oak.

REBEL YELL

US

Heaven Hill Distillery,
1701 West Breckinridge Street,
Louisville, Kentucky
www.rebelyellbourbon.com

Made at the Bernheim Distillery in Louisville, Rebel Yell is distilled with a percentage of wheat in its mashbill, instead of rye. Whiskey was first made to the Rebel Yell recipe in 1849 and, after enjoying popularity in the southern states for many years, the brand was finally released on an international basis during the 1980s. In addition to the standard bottling, the Rebel Yell range now includes American Whiskey and Small Batch, as well as a Small Batch Reserve.

◀ REBEL YELL

BOURBON 40% ABV

A nose of honey, raisins, and butter leads into a big-bodied bourbon, which again features honey and a buttery quality, along with plums and soft leather. The long finish is spicier than might be expected from the palate.

REDBREAST

Ireland

Midleton Distillery, Midleton,
County Cork
www.redbreastwhiskey.com

Redbreast was the name that
wine merchants Gilbey's gave
to the Jameson whiskey that they
matured and bottled. The bonded
trade was finally phased out in
1968, but Redbreast was so
popular that it was allowed to
continue well into the 1980s.
In the 1990s, Irish Distillers
bought the brand from Gilbey's
and relaunched the drink as a
12-year-old pure pot still, part-
matured in sherry wood. There are
also now 12-year-old cask strength
and 15- and 21-year-old versions.

REDBREAST 12-YEAR-OLD ▶
PURE POT STILL 40% ABV
This is, without doubt, one of the
world's finest whiskies. Flavors range
from ginger to cinnamon, peppermint
to linseed, and licorice to camphor.
A sherry note sets off an elegant finish.

REISETBAUER

Austria
*Zum Kirchdorfergut 1,
4062 Kirchberg-Thening
www.reisetbauer.at*

Hans Reisetbauer made his name as a quality distiller of fruit. He started distilling whisky in 1995, claiming—along with Waldviertler Roggenhof Distillery (*see p360*)—to be the first Austrian to do so. Reisetbauer grows his own barley, and does his own malting and fermentation. The wash is double distilled, and he uses Trockenbeerenauslese and Chardonnay casks, allowing the spirit to absorb traces of fruit left in the wood. His first bottling was released in 2002.

◀ REISETBAUER 7-YEAR-OLD
SINGLE MALT 43% ABV
Delicate and multilayered on the nose, with roasted aromas reminiscent of hazelnuts and dried herbs. Pleasant notes of bread and cereals on the palate. Slightly smoky, with fine spice.

REISETBAUER 12-YEAR-OLD
MALT 48% ABV
Similar to the 7-year-old, with greater emphasis on fruit notes from the wine barrels used for maturation.

RIDGEMONT

US

*Tom Moore Distillery, 1 Barton Road,
Bardstown, Kentucky*

When this bourbon was introduced
to the market in 2004, it was
initially called Ridgewood Reserve
but, after litigation between the
distillers and Woodford Reserve's
owners Brown-Forman, the name
was changed. The "1792" element
of the name pays homage to the
year in which Kentucky became
a state.

1792 RIDGEMONT RESERVE ▶

BOURBON 46.85% ABV

This comparatively delicate and
complex 8-year-old small-batch
bourbon boasts a soft nose with
vanilla, caramel, leather, rye, corn,
and spice notes. Oily and initially
sweet on the palate, caramel and
spicy rye develop along with a
suggestion of oak. The finish is
oaky, spicy, and quite long, with
a hint of lingering caramel.

RITTENHOUSE RYE

US

Heaven Hill Distillery,
1701 West Breckinridge Street,
Louisville, Kentucky
www.heavenhill.com

Once associated with Pennsylvania, the rye-whiskey making heartland, Rittenhouse Rye now survives in Kentucky, and its mashbill comprises 51 percent rye, 37 percent corn, and 12 percent barley.

Rittenhouse was launched by the Continental Distilling Company of Philadelphia soon after Prohibition was repealed in 1933, and was later acquired by Heaven Hill, which continued to produce the brand through the lean years when rye whiskey as a style was largely forgotten.

◀ **RITTENHOUSE STRAIGHT RYE**
RYE WHISKEY 40% ABV

Immediate aromas of rye, with black pepper, spice, and cedar. Oily on the palate, with more spicy rye, ginger, and vanilla, leading to cinnamon notes.

ROBERT BURNS

Scotland
Owner: Isle of Arran Distillers
www.arranwhisky.com

With the Scotch whisky industry
generally apt to employ Scottish
imagery and heritage associations
at the drop of a tam-o'-shanter, it is
a surprise to find that no one had
previously marketed a brand named
after Scotland's national bard.
Independent distiller Isle of Arran
(*see The Arran Malt, p23*) has
worked with the World Burns
Federation to fill this gap, and now
produces an officially endorsed
Burns Collection of blended
whiskies and malts.

ROBERT BURNS BLEND ▶
BLEND 40% ABV
Hints of oak on the nose give way to
sherry, almonds, toffee, and ripe fruits.
Plenty of toffee, cake, and dried fruits
on the palate, with a light to medium,
spicy finish.

ROBERT BURNS SINGLE MALT
SINGLE MALT 40% ABV
A nose of green apples, the acidity
tempered by a note of vanilla.
Apple and citrus notes on the palate,
balanced by vanilla again. An apéritif
whisky that is light in style and finish.

297

ROCK TOWN

US

1216 E 6th Street,
Little Rock, Arkansas
www.rocktowndistillery.com

Founded in 2010 by Phil
Brandon, Rock Town is the
first legal distillery in the state
of Arkansas since Prohibition. All
corn, wheat, and rye used in the
distilling process is grown within
a maximum of 125 miles (200km)
of the distillery. Rye and Hickory-
smoked whiskeys are made here,
along with Arkansas' first ever
bourbon, which is matured in
small, newly charred oak barrels
that were coopered in Arkansas
at Gibbs Brothers Cooperage. All
bottling takes place at the distillery.

◀ ROCK TOWN
ARKANSAS BOURBON

BOURBON 46% ABV

The nose is smoky and sweet, with
roasted corn aromas, while the palate
is smooth and sweet, with almonds
and digestive biscuits.

ROGUE SPIRITS

US

Rogue Brewery, 1339 NW Flanders, Portland, Oregon

www.rogue.com

Dead Guy Ale was created in the early 1990s to celebrate the Mayan Day of the Dead (November 1, or All Souls' Day) and, in 2008, the Oregon-based producers launched their Dead Guy Whiskey. It is distilled using the same four malts used in the creation of Dead Guy Ale, and fermented wort from the brewery is taken to the nearby Rogue House of Spirits, where it is double-distilled in a 150-gallon (570-liter) copper pot still. A brief maturation period follows, using charred American white-oak casks.

DEAD GUY ▶

BLENDED MALT 40% ABV
Youthful on the nose, with notes of corn, wheat, and fresh, juicy orange. The palate is medium-dry, fruity, and lively. Pepper and cinnamon feature in the finish.

ROSEBANK

Scotland
Camelon, Falkirk

Few Scottish distilleries have managed to stay in continuous production. Many closed during the 1980s and '90s when the industry was dealing with oversupply. Whether a distillery survived when demand picked up depended largely on location. Rosebank, near Falkirk, was closed in 1993 and has since been redeveloped. Founded in 1840, it was chosen to be part of The Ascot Malt Cellar in 1982. Unfortunately for Rosebank, when this became the "Classic Malts" series, Glenkinchie was picked to represent the Lowlands rather than Rosebank.

◀ ROSEBANK DOUGLAS LAING 16-YEAR-OLD

SINGLE MALT: LOWLANDS 50% ABV
This independent bottling from Douglas Laing is part of its Old Malt Cask collection. Despite its strength and age, it is fresh and citrusy.

ROYAL BRACKLA

Scotland
Cawdor, Nairn, Nairnshire

Brackla was founded between the
River Findhorn and the Murray
Firth by Captain William Fraser
in 1812. He was soon complaining
that, although he was surrounded
by whisky-drinkers, he could only
sell 100 gallons (450 liters) a year.
By way of compensation, he
secured the first royal warrant
for a distillery in 1835. Whether
he would recognize Royal Brackla
today seems unlikely: it was fully
modernized in the 1970s and 1990s
and now belongs to Bacardi, who
launched 12-, 16-, and 21-year-old
expressions in 2015.

ROYAL BRACKLA 12-YEAR-OLD ▶
SINGLE MALT: HIGHLANDS 40% ABV
Ripe peaches, spice, walnuts, malt,
honey, vanilla, and a slightly herbal
note on the nose. Spice, sweet sherry,
and mildly smoky orchard fruit on
the full palate, closing with cocoa
and ginger.

301

ROYAL CHALLENGE

India

Owner: United Spirits
www.unitedspirits.in

This "blend of rare Scotch and matured Indian malt whiskies" is owned by Shaw Wallace, a part of United Spirits since 2005. It is described as "the iconic" premium Indian whisky and, until 2008, it was also the bestselling premium Indian whisky, but is now severely challenged by Blenders Pride (*see p56*).

◄ ROYAL CHALLENGE

BLEND 42.8% ABV

A soft, rounded nose, with traces of malt, nuts, caramel, and a light rubber note. These aromas translate well in the taste at full strength. With water, it remains dense and full-bodied but the taste, diluted, is not as heavy. Very sweet, slightly nutty, and mouth-drying, but with a longish finish.

ROYAL LOCHNAGAR

Scotland
Ballater, Aberdeenshire
www.malts.com

This charming distillery sits alone on Deeside as the only whisky-making business in the area. It was founded in 1845 by John Begg, who wasted no time in asking his new neighbors at Balmoral Castle—Queen Victoria and Prince Albert—to look around his distillery, thereby adding the "Royal" to its name. In 2013, a Triple Matured bottling was released exclusively to Friends of the Classic Malts.

ROYAL LOCHNAGAR 12-YEAR-OLD ▶
SINGLE MALT: HIGHLANDS 40% ABV
A subtle, leathery nose with a flavor that becomes drier and more acidic before a spicy, sandalwood finish.

ROYAL LOCHNAGAR DISTILLERS EDITION 2000
SINGLE MALT: HIGHLANDS 48% ABV
Pears poached in dessert wine on the malty, gingery nose. The rich palate offers ripe peaches, figs, ginger, and cloves, closing with nutty spice.

ROYAL SALUTE

Scotland
Owner: Chivas Brothers
www.royalsalute.com

Originally produced by Seagram in 1953 to commemorate the coronation of Queen Elizabeth II, Royal Salute claims to be the first super-premium whisky.

Historically, Chivas Brothers were noted for their exceptional stocks of rare, aged whiskies, and these formed the basis for the Royal Salute expressions. Now controlled by Pernod Ricard, the blenders, led by the highly respected Colin Scott, have access to single malts from well-known distilleries like Glenlivet, Aberlour, Strathisla, and Longmorn.

◀ ROYAL SALUTE 21-YEAR-OLD
BLEND 40% ABV
Soft, fruity aromas balanced with a delicate floral fragrance and mellow, honeyed sweetness.

ROYAL SALUTE, THE HUNDRED CASK SELECTION
BLEND 40% ABV
Elegant, creamy, and exceptionally smooth, with a mellow, oaky, slightly smoky finish.

RUSSELL'S RESERVE

US

*Boulevard Distillery,
Lawrenceburg, Kentucky*

Austin Nichols' Master Distiller
Jimmy Russell and his son Eddie,
of Wild Turkey fame (*see p368*),
developed this small batch rye
whiskey, launched in 2007.
According to Eddie Russell,
"we knew the whiskey we wanted,
but had never tasted it before.
This one really makes the grade—
deep character and taste and,
at six years, aged to perfection."

RUSSELL'S RESERVE RYE ▶

RYE WHISKEY 45% ABV

Fruity, with fresh oak and almonds on
the nose. Full-bodied and robust, yet
smooth. Almonds, pepper, and rye
dominate the palate, while the finish is
long, dry, and characteristically bitter.

RUSSELL'S RESERVE
10-YEAR-OLD

BOURBON 45% ABV

This bourbon boasts a nose of soft
leather, pine, vanilla, and caramel. More
vanilla, toffee, almond, honey, and
coconut in the mouth, and a slightly
unusual note of chilis that continues
through the lengthy, spicy finish.

SAM HOUSTON

US

McLain & Kyne Ltd. (Castle Brands),
Louisville, Kentucky
www.samhoustonwhiskey.com

McLain & Kyne Ltd. is best known for what it terms "very small batch bourbons," and the firm blends whiskey from as few as eight to twelve barrels of varying ages for their Jefferson's (see p200) and Sam Houston bourbon brands.

Sam Houston was introduced in 1999 and is named after the colorful 19th-century soldier, statesman, and politician Samuel Houston, who became the first president of the Republic of Texas.

◀ SAM HOUSTON AMERICAN STRAIGHT WHISKEY

AMERICAN WHISKEY 43% ABV

Apples and a hint of caramel on the relatively light nose, while the palate is very sweet, with more caramel and emerging black pepper.

SAZERAC RYE

US

Buffalo Trace Distillery,
1001 Wilkinson Boulevard,
Frankfort, Kentucky
www.sazerac.com

Sazerac Rye is part of the annually updated Buffalo Trace Antique Collection and, having been aged for 18 years, is the oldest rye whiskey currently available. According to Buffalo Trace, the 18-year-old 2008 release is comprised of whiskey that has been aging in its warehouse on the first floor—this location enables the barrels to age slowly and gracefully.

SAZERAC RYE 18-YEAR-OLD ▶
RYE WHISKEY 45% ABV
Rich on the nose, with maple syrup and a hint of menthol. This expression is oily on the palate, fresh, and lively, with fruit, pepper, and pleasing oak notes. The finish boasts lingering pepper, with returning fruit and a final flavor of molasses.

SCAPA

Scotland
St. Ola, Orkney
www.scapamalt.com

Founded in 1885 on "Mainland," the largest of the Orkney islands, Scapa kept going more or less continuously until 1994, when it was shut down. Although production resumed three years later, it was only on a seasonal basis, using staff from its neighbor, Highland Park. For years it seemed there was only room for one viable distillery on Orkney—that being Highland Park—but Scapa's rescue came in the form of Allied Domecq, and over $3.7m was lavished on it in 2004. The company has since been bought by Chivas Brothers.

◀ SCAPA 14-YEAR-OLD
SINGLE MALT: ISLANDS 40% ABV
Compared to the robust, smoky Highland Park, Scapa is softer and a little sweeter. It has a heathery, dried-fruit character with a gentle spiciness.

SCOTTISH LEADER

Scotland
Owner: Burn Stewart Distillers
www.scottishleader.com

The owner describes Scottish Leader as an "international award-winning blend with a honey rich smooth taste profile. It has a growing presence in a number of world markets." The blend's heart is Deanston single malt, from the Perthshire distillery of the same name. Although it was initially targeted at the value-conscious supermarket buyer, Scottish Leader has subsequently been repackaged and moved somewhat upmarket. Today, there are Original, Signature, Supreme, and 12-year-old expressions.

SCOTTISH LEADER ▶
BLEND 40% ABV
A standard blend in which the flavor characteristics are tightly integrated. Not much to mark it out, but okay for mixing or drinking on the rocks.

SEAGRAM'S

Canada
Diageo Canada, West Mall, Etobicoke, Ontario

Joseph Emm Seagram ran a flour mill in Ontario in the 1860s, where he became interested in distilling as a way of using surplus grains. By 1883 distilling was the core business and Seagram was the sole owner. The brand 83 commemorates this. The V.O. brand stands for "Very Own" and was once the bestselling Canadian whisky in the world. Diageo now controls the Canadian Seagram's labels, as well as Seagram's 7 Crown (*see opposite*), which is marketed as an American whiskey.

◀ SEAGRAM'S V.O.
BLEND 40% ABV

The nose presents pear drops, caramel, and some rye spice, along with butter. Light-bodied, sweet, and lightly spicy, with a slightly acerbic mouthfeel.

SEAGRAM'S 83
BLEND 40% ABV

At one time, this was even more popular than V.O. Now it is a standard Canadian: smooth and easy to drink.

SEAGRAM'S 7 CROWN

US
Angostura Distillery,
Lawrenceburg, Indiana

One of the best known and most characterful blended American whiskeys, Seagram's 7 Crown has survived the break-up of the Seagram distilling empire and is now produced by Caribbean-based Angostura (of Angostura Bitters fame). This relative newcomer to the US distilling arena has acquired the former Seagram distillery at Lawrenceburg, where 7 Crown is made. The Lawrenceburg distillery is the largest spirits facility in the US in terms of production capacity.

SEAGRAM'S 7 CROWN ▶
BLEND 40% ABV
This possesses a delicate nose with a hint of spicy rye, and is clean and well structured on the spicy palate.

311

SHEEP DIP

Scotland

Owner: Spencerfield Spirits
www.spencerfieldspirit.com

Sheep Dip is one of the better blended malts. The brand has been around since the 1970s but, under the ownership of Whyte & Mackay, was largely ignored. In 2005, it was taken on by Alex and Jane Nicol, who aim to rebuild the former glory of so-called "orphan brands." Since then, they've introduced new packaging, appointed a global network of agents and, most important of all, reformulated the whisky under the guidance of master blender Richard Paterson. It seems to be working. The whiskies are aged between 8 and 12 years in quality first-fill wood, producing a great dram.

◀ SHEEP DIP

BLENDED MALT 40% ABV
The nose is delicate and refined. Great finesse on the palate, then a majestic assertion of pure malty flavors.

SIGNATURE

India
Owner: United Spirits
www.diageoindia.com

The recently introduced Signature
Rare Aged Whisky comes from the
McDowell's stable, owned by
United Spirits, and has the slogan
"Success is Good Fun." It is a
blend of Scotch and Indian malt
whiskies and is the fastest-growing
brand in the company's portfolio.
It has also won a clutch of
international awards, including a
gold in the Monde Selection 2006.

SIGNATURE ▶
BLEND 42.8% ABV
A rich nose, with a distinct medicinal
note. Straight, the taste is surprisingly
sweet, with smoky and medicinal
undertones, becoming less sweet with
water. Relatively light in body, with
a distinct peaty, smoky edge.

SLYRS

Germany

*Bayrischzellerstrasse 13 , 83727
Schliersee, Ortsteil Neuhaus
www.slyrs.de*

Slyrs was founded in 1999 and
makes a credible whisky, which
is distributed by Lantenhammer,
a schnapps distillery located in
the same village. Slyrs is bottled
after maturing for an unspecified
time in new American white-oak
barrels. In October 2008, Raritas
Diaboli, a special cask-strength
edition, was launched.

◄ SLYRS

SINGLE MALT 43% ABV

Some flowery aromas and spicy notes
deliver a nice and easy dram. The taste
varies according to the vintage.

SMÖGEN

Sweden

Smögen Whisky AB,
Ståleröd Ljungliden 1,
456 93 Hunnebostrand
www.smogenwhisky.se

Smögen, a farm-based distillery
on the west coast of Sweden,
started producing whisky in 2010.
Designed by its owner, lawyer and
whiskey aficionado, Pär Caldenby,
it has a 200-gallon (900-liter) wash
still and a 130-gallon (600-liter)
spirit still, with an annual capacity
of some 7,700 gallons (35,000 liters).
Caldenby imports heavily peated
malt from Scotland.

Smögen's first release, Smögen
Primör, came in 2013. It is a
3-year-old cask strength matured
in European oak and ex-Bordeaux
wine casks.

SMÖGEN PRIMÖR ▶

SINGLE MALT 63.7% ABV
Earthy nose of sweet smoke, salt,
leather, and cocoa. Sweet peat on
the palate, with berries and spices.

SOMETHING SPECIAL

Scotland
Owner: Chivas Brothers

It's quite a name to live up to, but "something special" is a justifiable claim for this premium blend, which is the third bestselling whiskey in South America, with sales of over half a million cases. The blend dates back to 1912, when it was created by the directors of Hill, Thomson & Co. of Edinburgh. The primary component is drawn from Speyside malts, especially the highly regarded Longmorn, which is at the heart of the blend. A 15-year-old version was launched in 2006. The distinctive bottle is said to have been inspired by an Edinburgh diamond-cutter.

◄ SOMETHING SPECIAL
BLEND 40% ABV
A distinctive blend of dry, fruity, and spicy flavors, with a subtle, smoky sweetness on the palate.

SPEY

Scotland

Glen Tromie, Kingussie,
Inverness-shire
www.speysidedistillery.co.uk

With a production of just 130,000 gallons (600,000 liters), the Speyside distillery, named after Scotland's biggest malt whisky region, is no giant. Nor is it all that old. Despite its rustic appearance—only a discreet modern smoke stack belies its youth—Speyside was commissioned in 1962 by the blender and bottler George Christie. Built stone-by-stone, it was not finished until 1987. In 2012, the distillery was acquired by Harvey's of Edinburgh, and, since 2015, its single malt has been marketed as Spey.

SPEY 12-YEAR-OLD ▶
SINGLE MALT: SPEYSIDE 40% ABV
Fresh and relatively light on the nose, with roasted barley, cooking apples, and nutty vanilla. More vanilla on the palate, along with walnuts, dried fruit, and brittle toffee.

SPEYBURN

Scotland
Rothes, Aberlour, Morayshire
www.inverhouse.com

Whether she knew it or not, Queen Victoria's loyal subjects at the newly built Speyburn Distillery near Rothes labored through the night to produce a whisky for her Diamond Jubilee in 1897. It was mid-December and, though the windows were not yet in place and snow was swirling in from outside, the distillery manager ordered the stills to be fired up. Speyburn has retained its Victorian charm and, since 1991, has been owned by Inver House.

◀ SPEYBURN 10-YEAR-OLD

SINGLE MALT: SPEYSIDE 40% ABV
Despite the release of older expressions, including a 25-year-old Solera, the core expression of Speyburn remains the 10-year-old, which has a flavor of vanilla fudge and a sweet, lingering finish.

SPRINGBANK

Scotland
Campbeltown, Argyll
www.springbankwhisky.com

Springbank was officially founded in 1823, at a time when there were no fewer than 13 licensed distillers in Campbeltown. Although this end of the Mull of Kintyre still feels pretty cut off by car, it was always a short hop across the Firth of Clyde to Glasgow by ship. And, as the second city of the British empire boomed, distilleries like Springbank were on hand to quench its ever-growing thirst. In the other direction there was the US but, when that went dry during Prohibition, and the big ☞

SPRINGBANK 12-YEAR-OLD CASK STRENGTH 2014 RELEASE ▶
SINGLE MALT: CAMPBELTOWN
54.3% ABV
Vanilla and sherry on the nose. The palate is earthy, with soft peat smoke, spice, ginger, caramel, and light sherry.

SPRINGBANK 10-YEAR-OLD
SINGLE MALT: CAMPBELTOWN
46% ABV
A complex cocktail of flavors: ripe citrus fruit, peat smoke, vanilla, and a faint underlying salty tang.

SPRINGBANK

blenders turned ever more to Speyside, Campbeltown's demise was swift. Yet Springbank survived, most likely thanks to its continuity: the Mitchells have been in charge since the mid-19th century, and have built up a real cult following for their innovative range of single malts.

Springbank malts all its own barley requirements in house on a traditional malting floor. It then mashes in a cast iron open mash tun, and the wash still is both directly fired and internally steam heated. The mature spirit is bottled on site.

◀ SPRINGBANK 18-YEAR-OLD

SINGLE MALT: CAMPBELTOWN
46% ABV

The nose is rich, with sweet cherry, angelica, and apricots, while the rounded palate offers fresh fruit, molasses, smoke, and licorice, leading into a slowly drying finish.

SPRINGBANK 15-YEAR-OLD

SINGLE MALT: CAMPBELTOWN
46% ABV

Sweet toffee and candied peel on the nose give way to more exotic sweet-and-sour flavors in the mouth.

ST. GEORGE

US

St. George Spirits, 2601 Monarch Street, Alameda, California
www.stgeorgespirits.com

St. George Spirits was established by Jörg Rupf in 1982, and the distillery operates two Holstein copper pot stills. A percentage of heavily roasted barley is used, some of which is smoked over alder and beech wood. Most of the single malt whiskey is put into former bourbon barrels and matured for between three and five years, with a proportion matured in French oak and former port casks.

ST. GEORGE ▶
SINGLE MALT 43% ABV
The nose offers fresh, floral notes, with fruit, nuts, coffee, and vanilla. It is quite delicate on the palate; sweet, nutty, and fruity, with a hint of menthol and cocoa. Vanilla and chocolate notes in the finish, along with gentle smoke.

STEWARTS CREAM OF THE BARLEY

Scotland
Owner: Chivas Brothers

First produced around 1831, this old-established brand is today a bestseller in Ireland. For many years it enjoyed great popularity in Scotland, too, not least because of its widespread distribution in the public house chain of Allied, the owner at the time. Single malt from Glencadam used to be at the heart of the blend. With changes in ownership, Glencadam is now in other hands, but the blend reputedly still contains a healthy proportion of up to 50 different single malts.

◄ STEWARTS CREAM OF THE BARLEY

BLEND 40% ABV

A malty, sweet, soft, and slightly spirity nose. The fruitiness of a young spirit on the palate—raw and a little smoky. Peppery, drying, charred-wood finish.

STRANAHAN'S

US

Stranahan's Colorado Whiskey,
2405 Blake Street, Denver, Colorado
www.stranahans.com

Jess Graber and George Stranahan established the Denver distillery, the first licensed distillery in Colorado, in March 2004. Whiskey is produced using a four-barley fermented wash produced by the neighboring Flying Dog Brewery. The distillation takes place in a Vendome still, and the spirit is put into new, charred American oak barrels. It is aged for a minimum of two years, and each bottled batch is composed of the contents of between two and six barrels.

STRANAHAN'S COLORADO WHISKEY ▶

COLORADO WHISKEY 47% ABV
The nose is very bourbon-like, with notes of caramel, licorice, spice, and oak. The palate is slightly oily, big, and sweet, with honey and spices. The fairly short finish is quite oaky.

STRATHISLA

Scotland
Keith, Banffshire
www.maltwhiskydistilleries.com

In 1786, Alexander Milne and
George Taylor founded the
Milltown Distillery in Keith. The
whisky it produced was known
as Strathisla and, in 1951, this
was adopted as the name for
the distillery. Over the years,
Strathisla has survived fires,
explosions, and bankruptcy, to
become the oldest and possibly
most handsome distillery in the
Highlands, with a high-gabled
roof and two pagodas. Bought by
Chivas Brothers in 1950, it has
been the spiritual home of Chivas
Regal ever since.

◄ **STRATHISLA 12-YEAR-OLD**
SINGLE MALT: SPEYSIDE 43% ABV
This has a rich, sumptuous nose and
a spicy, fruitcake character, thanks to
the influence of sherry. It is medium-
bodied, with a slight smoky note on
the finish.

STRATHMILL

Scotland
Keith, Banffshire
www.malts.com

With its twin pagoda roof, this handsome late-Victorian distillery was built in 1891 as the Glenisla-Glenlivet Distillery. Four years later it was bought by Gilbey's, the London-based gin distiller, and re-christened Strathmill—a reference to the fact that it stood on the site of an old corn mill. A single malt expression was released as early as 1909, but Strathmill's long-term role in life was—and is—to supply malt for blended Scotch, particularly J&B.

STRATHMILL FLORA & FAUNA 12-YEAR-OLD ▶

SINGLE MALT: SPEYSIDE 43% ABV
On the lighter, more delicate side of Speyside, Strathmill has a nutty, malty character with notes of vanilla from the wood. It is quite soft and medium-sweet on the tongue.

SULLIVANS COVE

Australia

Tasmania Distillery, Lamb Place, Cambridge, Tasmania
www.sullivanscove.com

In 1994, a small distillery was established in what is now Hobart. The malt whisky produced took the area's original name: Sullivan's Cove. The distillery changed hands in 2003, when it was moved to Cambridge, on the outskirts of Hobart. Locally grown, unpeated Franklin barley-malt is used. The spirit is distilled in a Charentais-style pot still, and bottled from single casks by hand. The whisky is now winning national awards.

◀ SULLIVANS COVE AMERICAN OAK CASK

SINGLE MALT 47.5% ABV
The initially sweet nose develops pepper and oaky notes. The palate has malt and vanilla.

SULLIVANS COVE DOUBLE CASK

SINGLE MALT 40% ABV
Vanilla, orange, lemon, honey, figs, and allspice on the nose. The mildly herbal palate delivers honey, ginger, dried fruits, then white pepper in the finish.

SUNTORY HAKUSHU

Japan
Torihara 2913–1, Hakushucho,
Komagun, Yamanashi
www.suntory.co.jp

Located in a forest high in the
Japanese Alps, Hakushu was once
the largest malt distillery in the
world, producing a vast array of
different makes for the Suntory
blenders; nowhere else offers such
an array of shapes and sizes of pot
stills. Hakushu single malt seems
to echo the location, being light,
gentle, and fresh.

SUNTORY HAKUSHU 12-YEAR-OLD ▶
SINGLE MALT 43.5% ABV
A very cool nose, with cut grass, a
growing mintiness, and a hint of
linseed oil. The palate is sweet but
quite slow; the minty, grassy character
is given depth by apricot fruitiness and
extra fragrance by a chamomile note.

SUNTORY HAKUSHU 18-YEAR-OLD
SINGLE MALT 43% ABV
Once again a vegetal note, this time
more like a tropical rain forest. There's
also plum, mango, hay, and fresh ginger.
Good acidity and a toasty, oaky finish.

327

Whiskey Tour:
JAPAN

Tokyo is a good starting point for the whiskey lover. The city has myriad whiskey bars and excellent train connections to the distilleries at Chichibu, Hakushu, and Gotemba. Further afield, Suntory's flagship distillery, Yamazaki, is also accessible by train, and can be combined with a visit to Kyoto or Osaka.

JAPAN

DAY 1: CHICHIBU DISTILLERY

❶ Chichibu, Japan's newest distillery, started by Ichiro Akuto, has no visitor facilities yet, but whiskey enthusiasts can arrange a personal tour by contacting the distillery in advance *(+81 (0)494 62 4601)*. Chichibu city is 90 minutes by train from Tokyo's Ikebukuro station. A taxi can be taken from the station to the distillery, which is outside the city.

Shinjiro Torii is revered in Japan as the founder of Suntory, which operates the Yamazaki and Hakushu distilleries on this tour.

TOUR STATISTICS

DAYS: 6
LENGTH: 530 miles (850km)
TRAVEL: Shinkansen (bullet trains), local trains
DISTILLERIES: 4

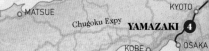

MATSUE

KYOTO

Chugoku Expy **YAMAZAKI** ❹

KOBE   OSAKA

FINISH

OKAYAMA

Sanyo Expy

HIROSHIMA

DAY 2: SUNTORY'S HAKUSHU DISTILLERY

② Hakushu is surrounded by a lovely nature reserve in the southern Japanese Alps. The nearest station is Kobuchizawa, which is 2 hours 30 minutes by express train (JR Chuo Line) from Tokyo's Shinjuku Station.

HAKUSHU DISTILLERY

DAYS 3–4: KIRIN'S GOTEMBA DISTILLERY

③ Gotemba is the start of one of the main routes up Mount Fuji, and home to Kirin's **Gotemba** Distillery. Many visitors come to visit both. They start climbing Fuji in the afternoon to reach the 8th or 9th stage by nightfall, where there are huts for pilgrims. The summit is reached at dawn. After descending, it is possible to get a bus back to Gotemba to visit the distillery. Although not the prettiest of distilleries, it has good facilities and a spectacular view of Fuji from its rooftop terrace.

MOUNT FUJI AND TRAIN

DAYS 5–6: SUNTORY'S YAMAZAKI DISTILLERY

YAMAZAKI DISTILLERY

④ It is best to take the bullet train to either Kyoto or Osaka to make a base for visiting the Suntory Distillery at **Yamazaki**, the company's original whisky-making plant. Local trains from either city stop at JR Yamazaki station. There are extensive visitor facilities, including an impressive tasting bar with exclusive bottlings. The distillery offers well-heeled clients a chance to buy a cask through its Owner's Cask scheme. There is also a traditional Shinto shrine to visit.

SENDAI

NIIGATA

FUKUSHIMA

Banetsu Expy

Hokuriku Expy

Tohoku Expy

Kanetsu Expy

NAGANO

START

① CHICHIBU

TOKYO

JR Chuo Line

IAKUSHU ②

HONSHU

JR Asian Line

GOTEMBA ③

Tokaido Shinkansen Line

GOYA

miles
0   30

0   30
kilometers

SUNTORY HIBIKI

Japan

Torihara 2913–1, Hakushucho,
Komagun, Yamanashi
www.suntory.co.jp

The fortunes of Suntory were built
on blended whiskies based on
malts from its two distilleries:
Yamazaki and Hakushu. Although
there is a move toward single
malts globally, the Hibiki range
is still regarded as very important.

◀ SUNTORY HIBIKI 17-YEAR-OLD

BLENDED MALT 43% ABV
This, the original Hibiki, has a soft,
generous nose featuring super-ripe
fruits, light peatiness, a hint of heavy
florals (jasmine), and citrus. On the
palate: caramel, black cherry, vanilla,
rosehip, and light oak structure.

SUNTORY HIBIKI 30-YEAR-OLD

BLENDED MALT 43% ABV
This multi-award winner is huge in
flavor, a compote of different fruits:
Seville orange, quince paste, quite
assertive wood, and walnuts, followed
by aniseed and fennel, and a deep
spiciness. The palate is sweet and
velvety, with Old English Marmalade
to the fore, with sweet, dusty spices.

SUNTORY YAMAZAKI

Japan
Yamazaki 5–2–2, Honcho,
Mishimagun, Osaka
www.suntory.co.jp

Established in 1923, Yamazaki claims to be the first malt distillery built in Japan, and was home to the fathers of the nation's whisky industry, Shinjiro Torii and Masataka Taketsuru. ☞

THE YAMAZAKI 12-YEAR-OLD ▶
SINGLE MALT 43% ABV
The mainstay of the range, the 12-year-old is crisp, with a fresh nose of pineapple, citrus, flowers, dried herbs, and a little oak. The palate is sweet and filled with ripe soft fruits and a hint of smoke.

THE YAMAZAKI 18-YEAR-OLD
SINGLE MALT 43% ABV
With age, Yamazaki acquires more influence from oak. The estery notes of younger variants are replaced by ripe apple, violet, and a deep, sweet oakiness. This impression continues on the palate with a mossy, pinelike character and the classic Yamazaki richness in the middle of the mouth. This is an extremely classy whisky.

331

SUNTORY YAMAZAKI

Like Hakushu, it produces a huge range of styles. The official single-malt bottlings concentrate on the sweet fruity expression. Single-cask bottlings have also been released. Most of the older expressions have been aged in ex-sherry casks, but there is the occasional Japanese-oak release for Japanese malt converts.

◀ THE YAMAZAKI DISTILLER'S RESERVE

SINGLE MALT 43% ABV

Fragrant and delicately fruity, with sandalwood on the nose. Summer fruits, vanilla, and subtle spice on the palate, with nutmeg and cinnamon at the close.

THE YAMAZAKI 25-YEAR-OLD

SINGLE MALT 43% ABV

A huge, concentrated, almost balsamic sherried nose, with sweet raisin, pomegranate, molasses, fig jam, prune, rose petal, musk, leather, and burning leaves. The palate is bitter and quite tannic. It's very dry.

TALISKER

Scotland
Carbost, Isle of Skye
www.taliskerwhisky.com

Talisker was founded on Skye
in 1830 by Hugh and Kenneth
MacAskill. Given the island's size
and proximity to the mainland, it
seems odd that it has traditionally
only had one distillery, when Islay
has so many.

Talisker struggled through the
19th century until, in 1898, it
teamed up with Dailuaine, then the
largest distillery in the Highlands.
In 1916, the joint venture was
taken over by a consortium
involving Dewar's, the Distillers
Company, and John Walker ☞

TALISKER 10-YEAR-OLD ▶
SINGLE MALT: ISLANDS 45.8% ABV
An iconic West Coast malt with a
pungent, slightly peaty character that
has a peppery catch on the finish.

TALISKER 18-YEAR-OLD
SINGLE MALT: ISLANDS 45.8% ABV
Age has softened the youthful vigor
of the 10-year-old, and given it a scent
of leather and aromatic smoke and a
creamy, mouth-filling texture.

TALISKER

 & Sons. Ever since, Talisker has been a key component in the Johnnie Walker Red Label.

Until 1928, Talisker was triple-distilled, like an Irish whiskey, which explains why two wash stills are paired to three spirit stills. The lyne arms have a unique U shape to increase reflux and produce a cleaner spirit, although the fact that this is then condensed in worm tubs seems contradictory, as worm tubs tend to produce a heavier, more sulphurous spirit. Whatever the rationale, it seems to work, and Talisker has won countless awards and fans.

◀ TALISKER DISTILLERS EDITION 1996

SINGLE MALT: ISLANDS 45.8% ABV
With a maturation that ends in Amoroso sherry casks, this whisky has a peppery, spicy character, softened by a luscious, dried-fruit richness in the mouth.

TALISKER 57° NORTH

SINGLE MALT: ISLANDS 57% ABV
Named in reference to the latitude of the distillery, this is rich, fruity, smoky, peppery, and spicy, with a long finish.

TAMDHU

Scotland

Knockando, Aberlour, Morayshire
Owner: Ian Macleod Distillers
www.tamdhu.com

Tamdhu is a large setup, with nine
pine washbacks, three pairs of
stills, and a mix of dunnage and
racked warehousing on site. The
former Saladin maltings, which
were an interesting feature of
Tamdhu, are now disused. Closed
in 2010, owners Edrington sold
the mothballed distillery to Ian
Macleod Distillers in 2011, with
production resuming the following
year. A 10-year-old with a strong
sherry cask maturation influence
is now the principal expression.

TAMDHU 10-YEAR-OLD ▶

SINGLE MALT: SPEYSIDE 40% ABV
Soft sherry notes on the nose. Citrus
fruit, gentle spice, and more sweet
sherry on the leathery palate, which
closes with black pepper.

TAMDHU BATCH STRENGTH (BATCH 1)

SINGLE MALT: SPEYSIDE 58.8% ABV
Vanilla, toffee, milk chocolate, and sweet
sherry on the nose. The palate offers
marmalade, malt, cinnamon, and pepper,
finishing with sherry and nutmeg.

TAMNAVULIN

Scotland

Ballindalloch, Banffshire
www.tamnavulinwhisky.com

In 1966, Invergordon Distillers, now part of Whyte & Mackay, decided to build a big new distillery in a picturesque corner of Upper Speyside by the River Livet. Its six stills could pump out as much as 880,000 gallons (4 million liters) of pure alcohol a year. Yet, in 1995, Tamnavulin closed down—the owners, it seemed, had decided to focus their attention on their other distilleries. The UB Group bought Whyte & Mackay in 2007, and now Tamnavulin is back up and running.

In 2016, the first new single malt in 20 years was launched in order to celebrate Tamnavulin's 50th anniversary.

◄ **TAMNAVULIN 12-YEAR-OLD**
SINGLE MALT: SPEYSIDE 40% ABV
A light, apéritif-style malt, with a dry, cereal character and minty nose. This standard release of the so-called "Stillman's Dram" is joined by occasional older expressions.

TANGLE RIDGE

Canada
Alberta Distillery, 1521 34th Avenue Southeast, Calgary, Alberta

This whisky from the Alberta Distillery (*see p13*) is sweeter than its stablemates, although, like the other Alberta whiskies, it is made exclusively from rye. Introduced in 1996, it is one of the new school of premium Canadian whiskies: aged 10 years in oak, it is then "dumped" and small amounts of vanilla and sherry are added. The spirit is then re-casked for a time to allow the flavors to marry.

Its name comes from a limestone wall in the Canadian Rockies that was discovered by distinguished explorer, artist, and writer Mary Schäffer (1861–1939).

**TANGLE RIDGE
DOUBLE CASK ▶**

CANADIAN RYE 40% ABV
Butterscotch and burned caramel on the nose, velvet-smooth mouthfeel, and a very sweet taste, with a hint of sherry. Lacks complexity, however.

TÉ BHEAG

Scotland
Owner: The Gaelic Whisky Co.
www.gaelicwhisky.com

Although it is blended and bottled elsewhere in Scotland, this is another brand from the Pràban na Linne company on Skye (The Gaelic Whisky Company). Té Bheag (pronounced *Chey Vek*) means "the little lady" and is the name of the boat in the logo. It is also colloquial Gaelic for a "wee dram." The blend is popular in France and has won medals in international competition.
Té Bheag is non–chill filtered, and Islay, Island, Highland, and Speyside malts aged from 8 to 11 years are used in the blend.

◄ TÉ BHEAG
BLEND 40% ABV
The nose is fresh, with a citrus note, good richness, a delicate peatiness, and a touch of cereal. Weighty on the palate, with a good touch of licorice, a toffeelike richness, and some peat.

TEACHER'S

Scotland
Owner: Beam Global
www.teacherswhisky.com

This venerable brand can be dated to 1830, when William Teacher opened a grocery shop in Glasgow. Like other whisky entrepreneurs, he soon branched out into the spirits trade. His sons took over, and blending became increasingly important. In 1884 the trademark Teacher's Highland Cream was registered, and this single brand eventually came to dominate the business. The whisky was always forceful in character, built around single malts from Glendronach and Ardmore. Today it continues to prove popular in South America.

TEACHER'S HIGHLAND CREAM ▶
BLEND 40% ABV
Full-flavored, oily, with fudge and caramel notes on the nose, and toffee and licorice on the palate. A well-rounded, smooth texture and a quick finish that leaves the palate refreshed.

TEANINICH

Scotland
Alness, Ross-shire
www.malts.com

Distillery visitors to the Highland village of Alness rarely notice Teaninich as they make their way to its more famous neighbor Dalmore. And yet Teaninich has been quietly distilling away almost constantly since 1817, when it was set up by Captain Hugh Munro.

Teaninich's role was to supply spirit for blending—no one was interested in marketing it as a single malt to whiskey-drinkers until 1992, when its owners, UDV, released a 10-year-old expression.

◄ TEANINICH FLORA & FAUNA 10-YEAR-OLD

SINGLE MALT: HIGHLANDS 43% ABV
The only official distillery bottling is polished and grassy, with a predominantly malty flavor.

TEANINICH GORDON & MACPHAIL 1991

SINGLE MALT: HIGHLANDS 46% ABV
A deep amber, fruitcake-flavored malt, with notes of mint, tobacco, cloves, and wood smoke.

TEELING

Ireland

Teeling Distillery,
13–17 Newmarket, Dublin 8
www.teelingwhiskey.com

When the $15 million Teeling
Distillery opened for business on
St. Patrick's Day 2015, it was the
first time since 1974 that whiskey
had been produced in Dublin.
The Teeling brothers wanted to
create a modern, city-based
distillery. It occupies two adjoining
converted warehouses and is
equipped with a four-ton mash
tun, six washbacks—two pine and
four stainless steel—and three pot
stills. The annual output is
currently 44,000 to 55,000 gallons
(200,000 to 250,000 liters).

TEELING SINGLE GRAIN ▶
SINGLE GRAIN 46% ABV
Sweet on the nose, with spicy fruit
notes. Notably spicy in the mouth,
with red berries and drying tannins.

TEELING SMALL BATCH
BLEND 46% ABV
Finished in ex-rum casks, it has vanilla
and spice on the nose, with sweet rum
in the background. Smooth and sweet,
with light, spicy wood notes.

341

TEERENPELI

Finland

Teerenpeli, Hämeenkatu 19, Lahti
www.teerenpeli.com

Teerenpeli Distillery began life in 1998 within a brewery in the city of Lahti, an hour north of Helsinki. In 2002, its owner, Anssi Pyysing, bought a restaurant nearby, and moved the distillery to the former parking ramp beneath it. The distillery used wash from the brewery until 2010, when a new mash tun was installed, as well as a new visitor center. The distillery is now the biggest in Finland, with a capacity of up to 8,800 gallons (40,000 liters) a year.

◀ TEERENPELI 3-YEAR-OLD NO. 001

SINGLE MALT 43% ABV
A lot of grain (barley), vanilla, and oak with a slightly thick body.

TEERENPELI 6-YEAR-OLD

SINGLE MALT 43% ABV
In Finnish, Teerenpeli means "flirtation." True to its name, this malt is soft and seductive, with pound cake and baked apple flavors, an intriguing mix of herbal and spice notes, and a spritzy mouthfeel.

TEMPLETON RYE

US

East 3rd Street, Templeton, Iowa
www.templetonrye.com

Scott Bush's Templeton Rye whiskey came onto the market in 2006. It is distilled in a 300-gallon (1,150-liter) copper pot still in Indiana before being aged in new, charred-oak barrels.

Bush boasts that his rye is flavored to a Prohibition-era recipe. During the years of the Great Depression, a group of farmers in the Templeton area started to distill a rye whiskey illicitly in order to boost their faltering agricultural incomes. Soon, "Templeton Rye" achieved a widespread reputation as a high quality spirit.

TEMPLETON RYE SMALL BATCH ▶

RYE WHISKEY 40% ABV
Bright, crisp, and mildly sweet on the palate. The finish is smooth, long, and warming.

THOMAS H. HANDY

US

Buffalo Trace Distillery,
1001 Wilkinson Boulevard,
Frankfort, Kentucky
www.buffalotrace.com

Thomas H. Handy Sazerac is the newest addition to the Buffalo Trace Antique Collection. It is an uncut and unfiltered straight rye whiskey, named after the New Orleans bartender who first used rye whiskey to make the Sazerac Cocktail. According to the distillers, the barrels are aged six years and five months on the fifth floor of Warehouse M—"it's very flavorful and will remind drinkers of fruitcake."

◀ **THOMAS H. HANDY SAZERAC 2008 EDITION**

RYE WHISKEY 63.8% ABV

Summer fruits and pepper notes on the nose. The palate is a blend of soft vanilla and peppery rye; the finish is long, with oily, spicy oak.

THREE SHIPS

South Africa
James Sedgwick Distillery,
Wellington East, Drakenstein 7655
www.threeshipswhisky.co.za

The James Sedgwick Distillery, named after businessman Captain James Sedgwick, was founded around 1886, though it has only been producing whisky since 1990. The distillery's Three Ships brand was originally a blend of imported Scotch and native South African whisky and this tradition has continued in the Select and Premium Select expressions. Other expressions include the limited edition 10-year-old Single Malt—South Africa's first single malt whisky—of which there have been three subsequent releases since its initial launch in 2003, and the Special Release, the first blend made entirely of South African whisky.

THREE SHIPS 10-YEAR-OLD ▶
SINGLE MALT 43% ABV
The nose is floral, with just a hint of brine, plus barley and fresh pears. The palate is rounded and malty, with ripe peaches, honey, and soft spices.

345

TINCUP

US
Tincup Whiskey, Denver, Colorado
www.tincupwhiskey.com

Tincup is the latest whiskey
venture of Colorado-based Jess
Graber, cofounder of Stranhan's
Whiskey Distillery. Although
Graber has been distilling whiskey
since 1972, the ex-construction
company boss, firefighter, and
rodeo rider more recently decided
he wanted to offer the market a
bourbon-style whiskey with a
more powerful, spicy flavor. The
result was Tincup, which has a
high rye content in its mashbill,
and is sourced from the MGP
Distillery at Lawrenceburg,
Indiana. The name recalls days
when gold prospectors drank
whiskey from tin cups.

◀ TINCUP AMERICAN WHISKEY
AMERICAN WHISKEY 40% ABV
Lots of spice on the nose, with
warm apple pie, honey, and ginger.
Cinnamon, toffee, and more apple on
the palate, with caramel and lively
spice in the finish.

TOBERMORY

Scotland

Tobermory, Isle of Mull
www.tobermory.co.uk

Tobermory's survival has been
a small miracle, given that it has
spent much of its life lying idle.

It was founded in the 1790s by
local businessman John Sinclair,
but closed on his death in 1837.
It was revived briefly in the 1880s,
but operation was sporadic and
it closed again between 1930
and 1972. Again, production
was sporadic until it was sold
to its present owners, Burn
Stewart Distillers in 1993.

TOBERMORY 10-YEAR-OLD ▶

SINGLE MALT: ISLANDS 40% ABV
This fresh, unpeated, maritime
malt claims to have a slight smoky
character, owing to the water from
Mull's peat lochans. If true, the effect
is subtle.

TOBERMORY 15-YEAR-OLD

SINGLE MALT: ISLANDS 46.3% ABV
The nose has rich fruitcake notes and
a trace of marmalade, thanks to aging
in sherry casks. The spicy character
comes through on the tongue. It is
non–chill filtered and cask strength.

GREAT WHISKEYS

T

TOMATIN

Scotland
Tomatin, Inverness-shire
www.tomatin.com

With 23 stills and a capacity of 2.6 million gallons (12 million liters) of pure alcohol, Tomatin was the colossus of the malt whisky industry in 1974, at the time of its expansion.

Founded in 1897, it took a while to reach its supersize status. Its two stills were increased to four as recently as 1956; thereafter, expansion was rapid until it peaked in the 1970s, just in time for the first big post-war slump. Tomatin struggled on as an independent distillery until 1985, when the liquidators arrived.

◀ TOMATIN 12-YEAR-OLD
SINGLE MALT: HIGHLANDS 40% ABV
A mellow, soft-centered Speyside-style malt, which replaced the old core 10-year-old expression back in 2003.

TOMATIN 18-YEAR-OLD
SINGLE MALT: HIGHLANDS 43% ABV
The deep amber hue betrays a strong sherry influence that brings out fruity and cinnamon flavors in the malt.

A year later it was sold to two of its long-standing customers—Takara Shuzo and Okara & Co—thus becoming the first Scottish distillery in Japanese hands.

With 11 fewer stills, production has been cut back to 1.1 million gallons (5 million liters), which still allows plenty of capacity for bottling as a single malt. Tomatin's principal bottlings include 12-, 18-, and 30-year-olds, and Legacy, the no-age-statement, while several expressions of peated Tomatin have been released since 2013 under the Cù Bòcan label.

TOMATIN LEGACY ▶
SINGLE MALT: HIGHLANDS 43% ABV
The fragrant nose offers malt, honey, pepper, and faint treacle. The palate is fresh and fruity, with pineapple, pepper, and a suggestion of chili in the drying finish.

TOMATIN 30-YEAR-OLD
SINGLE MALT: HIGHLANDS 49.3% ABV
A voluptuous after-dinner dram with a big, sherried nose and impressive legs.

349

TOMINTOUL

Scotland

Kirkmichael, Ballindalloch, Grampian
www.tomintoulwhisky.com

Tomintoul opened in 1964—a time of great confidence in the industry, with booming sales of blended Scotch. Its role in life was simply to supply malt for these blends. This role continues under Angus Dundee, who bought the distillery in 2000, when it was in need of malt for its own blends. While single malts account for a small fraction of the 600,000 gallons (3.3 million liters) produced each year, the number of expressions has increased greatly. The distillery's oldest expression is a 40-year-old released in 2015.

◄ TOMINTOUL 10-YEAR-OLD

SINGLE MALT: SPEYSIDE 40% ABV
This delicate, apéritif-style malt has some vanilla from the wood and a light cereal character.

TOMINTOUL 16-YEAR-OLD

SINGLE MALT: SPEYSIDE 40% ABV
Extra years give this expression a nuttier, spicier character with orange peel aromas, as well as more depth and a more rounded texture.

TORMORE

Scotland

Advie, Grantown-on-Spey, Morayshire
www.tormoredistillery.com

Built on a grand scale in 1958, Tormore symbolizes the whiskey industry's self-confidence at a time when global demand for blended Scotch was growing strongly. With its copper-clad roof and giant chimney stack, the distillery towers up beside the A95 in Speyside. It seems no expense was spared by the architect, Sir Albert Richardson, a past president of the Royal Academy. Tormore is now owned by Chivas Brothers (Pernod Ricard), who released 14- and 16-year-old variants in 2014.

TORMORE 14-YEAR-OLD ▶
SINGLE MALT: SPEYSIDE 40% ABV
Tangy berry fruits, vanilla, spice, and almonds on the nose. The palate is smooth and citric, with toffee, ginger, and a closing note of pepper.

351

TULLAMORE D.E.W.

Ireland
www.tullamoredew.com

In 1901, the worldwide sales of Irish whiskey peaked at 10 million cases, around the period that the Williams family gained control of Tullamore Distillery. D.E. Williams's name is still associated with the brand; as in Tullamore D.E.W-illiams. In 1954, the distillery was sold, ending up in the hands of William Grant & Sons Ltd in 2010, who built a large new distillery on the outskirts of Tullamore. After Jameson, Tullamore D.E.W. is the world's second-best-selling Irish whiskey.

◀ TULLAMORE D.E.W.
BLEND 40% ABV
This whiskey is fairly one-dimensional. It has a characteristic bourbon burn, with not much else to recommend it.

TULLAMORE D.E.W. 12-YEAR-OLD
BLEND 40% ABV
A considerable step up from the other Tullamore blends, this is reminiscent of a premium Jameson. The precious trinity of pot still, sherry, and oak is very much in evidence.

TULLIBARDINE

Scotland
Blackford, Perthshire
www.tullibardine.com

Tullibardine was a mothballed distillery until it was bought by an independent consortium in 2003 that began distilling again. In 2011, the French family drinks company Picard Vins & Spiritueux purchased Tullibardine, launching an entirely new product range in 2013. Two years later, the oldest cask of whisky in the Tullibardine warehouse—dating from 1952—was bottled as the first release in the Custodian Collection.

TULLIBARDINE 225 SAUTERNES FINISH ▶

SINGLE MALT: HIGHLANDS 43% ABV
Citrus fruits, vanilla, white pepper, and a slightly herbal note on the nose. Citrus fruits carry over onto the malty palate, with orange, milk chocolate, and enduring spice.

TULLIBARDINE SOVEREIGN

SINGLE MALT: HIGHLANDS 43% ABV
The floral nose features fudge, vanilla, and freshly cut, sweet grass, while the palate is fruity and malty with cocoa, vanilla, and a spicy finish.

TYRCONNELL

Ireland

Cooley Distillery, Riverstown,
Cooley, County Louth
www.kilbeggandistillingcompany.com

It would be hard to find anyone who remembers the original Old Tyrconnell whiskey. The distillery that produced it, Andrew A. Watt and Company of Derry City, closed in 1925. In its day, this whiskey (named after a race horse) was very popular in the US, and early film of baseball games at the Yankee Stadium show billboards advertising "Old Tyrconnel."

◄ TYRCONNELL SINGLE MALT
SINGLE MALT 40% ABV
Cooley's best-selling malt and it's easy to see why. This has the loveliest nose of any Irish whiskey, releasing jasmine, honeysuckle, and malted-milk cookies.

TYRCONNELL PORT CASK
SINGLE MALT 46% ABV
Port changes the nose slightly, spicing things up. The body has aromas of fig pastry and plum pudding.

But the combined effects of civil unrest in Ireland and Prohibition in the US pushed Watt and many other Irish distilleries into the hands of the (Scottish) Distillers Company Limited in 1922. To protect their core Scotch brands, DCL ruthlessly closed every Irish distillery they bought, bringing the industry across the island to its knees. However, The Tyrconnell was the first brand Dr. John Teeling, founder of Cooley Distillery, chose to bring back to life when he bottled his first single malt in 1992. The brand is now owned by Beam Suntory.

TYRCONNELL SHERRY CASK ▶

SINGLE MALT 46% ABV

The best of the wood finishes—malt and fruity sherry fuse beautifully.

TYRCONNELL MADEIRA CASK

SINGLE MALT 46% ABV

Madeira and Ireland do each other proud here. Warm hints of cinnamon and mixed spice dance on the palate.

VAN WINKLE

US
*2843 Brownsboro Road
Louisville, Kentucky
www.oldripvanwinkle.com*

The legendary Julian P. "Pappy" Van Winkle, Sr. was a salesman for W. L. Weller & Sons who went on to become famous for his Old Fitzgerald bourbon.

Van Winkle specializes in small-batch, aged whiskeys. The bourbons are made with wheat, rather than cheaper rye. This is said to give the whiskeys

◀ PAPPY VAN WINKLE'S FAMILY RESERVE 15-YEAR-OLD

BOURBON 53.5% ABV

A sweet caramel and vanilla nose, with charcoal and oak. Full-bodied, round, and smooth in the mouth, with a long and complex finish of spicy orange, toffee, vanilla, and oak.

OLD RIP VAN WINKLE 10-YEAR-OLD

BOURBON 45% ABV

Caramel and molasses on the big nose, then honey and rich, spicy fruit on the profound, mellow palate. The finish is long, with coffee and licorice notes.

a smoother, sweeter flavor during the long maturation period favored by Van Winkle. All the whiskeys are matured for at least 10 years in lightly charred mountain oak barrels.

Buffalo Trace *(see p66)* has been in partnership with Julian Van Winkle, "Pappy" Van Winkle's grandson, since 2002, making and distributing his whiskeys. The current expressions were produced at several distilleries, and matured at the Van Winkle's now silent Old Hoffman Distillery.

VAN WINKLE FAMILY RESERVE RYE 13-YEAR-OLD ▶

RYE WHISKEY 47.8% ABV

An almost uniquely aged rye. Powerful nose of fruit and spice. Vanilla, spice, pepper, and cocoa in the mouth. A long finish pairs caramel with black coffee.

PAPPY VAN WINKLE'S FAMILY RESERVE 20-YEAR-OLD

BOURBON 45.2% ABV

Old for a bourbon, this has stood the test of time. Sweet vanilla and caramel nose, plus raisins, apples, and oak. Rich and buttery in the mouth, with molasses and a hint of char. The finish is long and complex, with a touch of oak charring.

VAT 69

Scotland
Owner: Diageo

At its peak, VAT 69 was the 10th best-selling whisky in the world, and references to it crop up in films and books from the 1950s and '60s. It was launched in 1882 and was once the flagship brand of the independent South Queensferry blenders William Sanderson & Co, its name coming from the fact that VAT 69 was the finest of 100 possible blends tested. Today its current owner, Diageo, gives precedence to Johnnie Walker and J&B, and it might not be unreasonable to suggest that—despite sales of more than 1 million cases a year in Venezuela, Spain, and Australia—VAT 69's glory days are behind it.

◀ VAT 69
BLEND 40% ABV
A light and well-balanced standard blend with an initial, noticeably sweet impact of vanilla ice cream, and a pleasantly malty background.

W. L. WELLER

US

Buffalo Trace Distillery,
1001 Wilkinson Boulevard,
Frankfort, Kentucky
www.buffalotracedistillery.com

Distilled by Buffalo Trace,
W. L. Weller is made with wheat
as the secondary grain, for an
extra smooth taste.

William LaRue Weller was
a prominent 19th-century
Kentucky distiller, whose
company ultimately merged
with that of the Stitzel brothers
in 1935. A new Stitzel-Weller
Distillery was subsequently
constructed in Louisville.

W. L. WELLER SPECIAL RESERVE ▶

BOURBON 45% ABV

Fresh fruit, honey, vanilla, and toffee
characterize the nose, while the palate
has lots of flavor, featuring ripe corn
and spicy oak. The medium-length
finish displays sweet, cereal notes
and pleasing oak.

WALDVIERTLER

Austria
Whisky-Erlebniswelt J. Haider GmbH, 3664 Roggenreith 3
www.whiskyerlebniswelt.at

The Waldviertler Distillery makes two single malts—J. H. Single Malt and J. H. Special Single Malt "Karamell"— and three rye whiskies—J. H. Original Rye, J. H. Pure Rye Malt, and J. H. Special Pure Rye Malt "Nougat."

Waldviertler uses casks made from the local Manhartsberger oak trees. The whiskies are matured for three to twelve years and offered as single-cask bottlings. Other spirits made here are vodka, gin, and brandy, but—unusually for a European distillery—whisky is the main focus.

WALDVIERTLER J. H. SPECIAL PURE RYE MALT "NOUGAT" ▶
RYE WHISKY 41% ABV
A gentle, sweet taste of honey, harmonizing perfectly with the light vanilla taste.

WALDVIERTLER J. H. SPECIAL SINGLE MALT "KARAMELL"
SINGLE MALT 41% ABV
Smoky and dry, with an intense caramel flavor.

360

WAMBRECHIES

France

1 Rue de la Distillerie,
59118 Wambrechies,
Nord-Pas-de-Calais
www.wambrechies.com

Wambrechies was founded in 1817 as a *jenever* (gin) distillery and is one of only three stills left in the region. It continues to produce an impressive range of *jenevers*, as well as one malt whisky and a *jenever* beer. Wambrechies whiskies are bottled at three and eight years old, with the younger whisky consisting of a lighter, floral blend and the older having a deeper, spicy character. They have also released two 12-year-old expressions.

WAMBRECHIES 8-YEAR-OLD ▶
SINGLE MALT 40% ABV
Delicate nose, with aniseed, fresh paint, vanilla, and cereal notes. Smooth on the palate, with a fine, malty profile. Spicy finish, with powdered ginger and milk chocolate.

WHISKY CASTLE

Switzerland

Schlossstraße 17, 5077 Elfingen www. whisky-castle.com

Käsers Schloss (the Swiss name of the distillery) is owned by Ruedi and Franziska Käser. The couple started producing whisky in 2000 and expanded the business in 2006 to include themed events such as whisky dinners and whisky conferences at their premises. The brand name of their whisky in English is Whisky Castle, and there are a number of expressions, including Double Wood, Terroir, Smoke Barley (aged in new French oak casks), Smoke Rye, Full Moon, and Château (matured in Château d'Yquem wine casks).

◀ WHISKY CASTLE FULL MOON

SINGLE MALT 43% ABV

Made from smoked barley during the full moon, this is a young whisky with a sweetish aroma and taste.

WHITE HORSE

Scotland
Owner: Diageo

In its heyday, White Horse was one of the world's top ten whiskies, selling more than 2 million cases a year. Its guiding genius was "Restless" Peter Mackie, described in his day as "one-third genius, one-third megalomaniac, and one-third eccentric." He took over the family firm in 1890 and built an enviable reputation as a gifted blender and entrepreneur.

White Horse is still marketed in more than 100 countries. A deluxe 12-year-old version, White Horse Extra Fine, is occasionally seen.

WHITE HORSE ▶
BLEND 40% ABV
Complex and satisfying, White Horse retains the robust flavor of Lagavulin, assisted by renowned Speysiders such as Aultmore. With its long finish, this is a stylish, intriguing blend of crisp grain, clean malt, and earthy peat.

WHYTE & MACKAY

Scotland
www.whyteandmackay.co.uk

The Glasgow-based firm of Whyte
& Mackay started blending in
the late 19th century. Its flagship
Special brand quickly established
itself as a Scottish favorite, and
remains so to this day. Having been
through a bewildering number of
owners and a management buyout
in recent years, the company
was acquired in May 2007 by the
Indian conglomerate UB Group,
which sold it to Emperador Inc.
in 2014.

◄ WHYTE & MACKAY SPECIAL
BLEND 40% ABV
The nose is full, round, and well-
balanced. On the palate, honeyed
soft fruits in profusion; smooth and
rich, with a long finish.

WHYTE & MACKAY
THE THIRTEEN
BLEND 40% ABV
Full, firm, and rich nose, with a slight
hint of sherry wood. "Marrying" for
a full year before bottling gives great
backbone. A well-integrated blend.

One constant through all these changes has been highly regarded master blender, Richard Paterson, who joined the firm in 1970 and has received a great number of awards. As well as creating the "new" 40-year-old, Paterson has overseen several aged innovations.

The backbone of the blends emanates from Speyside and the Highlands. Dalmore and—to a lesser extent—Isle of Jura are the company's flagship single malts, and Dalmore's influence can be felt in the premium blends. All the blends are noticeably smooth and well-balanced.

WHYTE & MACKAY 30-YEAR-OLD ▶

BLEND 40% ABV

The flagship of the Whyte & Mackay range is a big, rich, oaky whisky with a deep mahogany hue. The sherry influence is strong, with a pepperiness mellowed by the sweeter flavors.

WHYTE & MACKAY OLD LUXURY

BLEND 40% ABV

A rich bouquet, with malty notes and a subtle sherry influence. It all blends smoothly on the palate. Mellow and silky textured. Warming finish.

THE WILD GEESE

Ireland
www.thewildgeese-irishwhiskey.com

The term "Wild Geese" refers to those Irish nobles and soldiers who left to serve in continental European armies from the late 17th century to the dawn of the 20th century.

The name has come down through history to embrace all the men and women who left Ireland in the last 400 years—not just the nobles. The idea of diaspora and emigration has, of course, been a poignant theme in Irish culture and remains so today. Wild Geese raises a glass to this part of Irish history, and they've produced a good whiskey for the job.

◀ THE WILD GEESE CLASSIC BLEND

BLEND 40% ABV

A hard candy nose. The malt doesn't have much impact here, leaving the grain to carry things to the finish.

THE WILD GEESE RARE IRISH

BLEND 43% ABV

A rich and malty blend, with some spiciness and lemon notes in the body. You'll find a little dry oak in the finish.

WILD TURKEY

US

*Boulevard Distillery, US Highway
62 East, Lawrenceburg, Kentucky
www.wildturkeybourbon.com*

The Boulevard Distillery is
situated on Wild Turkey Hill,
above the Kentucky River, near
Lawrenceburg. The distillery was
first established in 1905 by the
three Ripy brothers, whose family
had been making whiskey since
the year 1869. The Wild Turkey
brand itself was conceived in
1940, when Austin Nichols' ☞

WILD TURKEY 81 PROOF ▶
BOURBON 40.5% ABV
Spicy corn, vanilla, oak, and coffee
on the nose. The palate yields big
caramel and honey notes, plus
cinnamon and allspice.

WILD TURKEY 101 PROOF
BOURBON 50.5% ABV
Jimmy Russell maintains that 50.5%
ABV (101 proof) is the optimum
bottling strength for Wild Turkey.
This has a remarkably soft, yet rich,
aroma for such a high proof whiskey.
Fullbodied, rich, and robust palate,
with vanilla, fresh fruit, spice, brown
sugar, and honey. Oak notes develop
in the powerful, yet smooth, finish.

WILD TURKEY

 Thomas McCarthy chose a quantity of 101 proof straight bourbon from his company stocks to take along on a wild turkey shoot. Today, Wild Turkey is distilled under the watchful eyes of legendary Master Distiller Jimmy Russell, the world's longest-tenured active Master Distiller, and his son Eddie, who is the fourth generation Russell to work at the distillery. In 2015, Eddie was named Master Distiller in his own right after 35 years of working with the Wild Turkey brand.

◄ WILD TURKEY RARE BREED
BOURBON (VARIABLE ABV)
A complex, initially assertive nose, with nuts, oranges, spices, and floral notes. Honey, oranges, vanilla, tobacco, mint, and molasses make for an equally complex palate. A long, nutty finish, with spicy, peppery rye.

WILD TURKEY KENTUCKY SPIRIT
BOURBON 50.5% ABV
A fresh, attractive nose of oranges and notes of rye. Complex on the palate, with almonds, honey, toffee, more oranges, and a hint of leather. The finish is long, gradually darkening and becoming more treacly.

WILLIAM LAWSON'S

Scotland
Owner: John Dewar & Sons (Bacardi)

Although the Lawson's brand dates back to 1849, the "home" distillery today is MacDuff, built in 1960. Lawson's is managed alongside its big brother, Dewar's, and sells well over 1 million cases a year in France, Belgium, Spain, and parts of South America.

Glen Deveron single malt from MacDuff features heavily in the blend. MacDuff uses the highest percentage of sherry wood of any whisky in the Dewar's group, making the Lawson house style full in flavor and rich golden in color.

WILLIAM LAWSON'S FINEST ▶
BLEND 40% ABV
Slightly dry nose, with delicate oak notes. Well-balanced palate, with hints of crisp candy apple. With a medium to full body, this punches above its weight.

WILLIAM LAWSON'S SCOTTISH GOLD 12-YEAR-OLD
BLEND 40% ABV
Fuller-flavored than the standard Lawson's expression, suggesting a higher malt content.

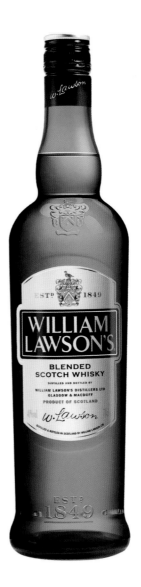

Whiskey Tour:
KENTUCKY

The state of Kentucky is the bourbon-producing heartland of the US and home to many of the best-known names in American whiskey. Most of the distilleries offer visitor facilities, allowing guests to study this historic spirit. Touring them is a great way to experience the beauty of Kentucky.

DAY 1: BUFFALO TRACE, WOODFORD RESERVE

BARRELS AT WOODFORD RESERVE

❶ Frankfort, the state capital, has a range of hotels and restaurants, and is the home of **Buffalo Trace**. The distillery's large visitor center offers tours throughout the year.

❷ **Woodford Reserve** lies near the attractive town of Versailles, in Kentucky's famous "bluegrass" horse-breeding country. Its copper pot stills are the highlight of the distillery tour.

DAY 2: WILD TURKEY, FOUR ROSES

❸ Spectacularly situated on a hill above the Kentucky River, **Wild Turkey's** Boulevard Distillery allows visitors into its production areas at most times of the year.

❹ **Four Roses** Distillery is a striking structure, built in the style of a Spanish Mission. Tours are available from autumn to spring (the distillery is closed throughout the summer). You can also pre-arrange to visit Four Roses' warehouse at Cox's Creek.

WILD TURKEY EMBLEM

LOUISVILLE

I-71

I-64

150

KENTUCKY

I-65

FINISH

❾ **JIM BEAM**

OSCAR GETZ

❼ ❻ ❺

BARTON
BARDSTOWN

HEAVEN HILL

Loretto Rd

❽

MAKER'S MARK

TOUR STATISTICS

DAYS: 5
LENGTH: 85 miles (137km)
TRAVEL: Car
DISTILLERIES: 8

DAY 3: HEAVEN HILL, BARTON, OSCAR GETZ

❺ Bardstown is renowned as the "World Capital of Bourbon," and makes an excellent base for visiting the distilleries in the area. Book a room at the Old Talbott Tavern, which offers a well-stocked bourbon bar. Then head out to the **Heaven Hill** Bourbon Heritage Center, which includes a tour of a bourbon-aging rackhouse and the chance to taste two Heaven Hill whiskeys.

HEAVEN HILL, BARDSTOWN

❻ The **Barton 1792 Distillery** in downtown Bardstown traditionally maintained a low profile compared to its neighbors, but nowadays comprehensive tours of the production areas are available, together with a state-of-the-art visitor center.

❼ A few blocks from Barton, the **Oscar Getz** Whiskey Museum houses a collection of whiskey artefacts, including rare antique bottles, a moonshine still, and Abraham Lincoln's original liquor licence.

DAY 4: MAKER'S MARK

❽ The historic **Maker's Mark** Distillery stands on the banks of Hardin's Creek, near Loretto, in Marion County. The distillery grounds are notable, being home to some 275 species of trees and shrubs. Guided distillery tours are available daily.

DAY 5: JIM BEAM

❾ **Jim Beam's** Clermont Distillery offers tours of the site grounds, a working rackhouse, and the Hartmann Cooperage Museum. The American Outpost is an onsite visitor center, with a film about the bourbon-making process at Jim Beam and displays of whiskey memorabilia that take in more than two centuries of bourbon history.

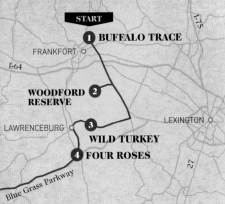

JIM BEAM'S CLERMONT DISTILLERY

WINDSOR

Scotland
Owner: Diageo

The name Windsor is an overt link to the British royal family, and the brand's packaging underlines its luxury position, especially in the highly competitive South Korean market. Windsor was originally developed in a partnership between Seagram and local Korean producer Doosan; later Diageo acquired the Seagram interest and launched Windsor 17 as the first super-premium whisky in 2000. Windsor 17's sweeping popularity in Korea posed a threat to its competitors, many of whom have since emulated the older style.

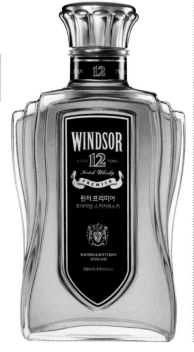

◄ WINDSOR 12-YEAR-OLD
BLEND 40% ABV
Vanilla, wood, and light fresh fruit on the nose. Green apples on the palate, with honey, more vanilla, and spiciness that mellows into a smooth finish.

WINDSOR 17-YEAR-OLD
BLEND 40% ABV
A rich vanilla crème brûlée nose, with fruit and a background layer of malt. Fresh fruit and honey on the palate, with creamy vanilla oak notes.

WINDSOR CANADIAN

Canada

Alberta Distillery, 1521 34th Avenue Southeast, Calgary, Alberta

One might think that this comes from the Hiram Walker Distillery in Windsor, Ontario; actually, it is made at the Alberta Distillery *(see p13)*. The name is no doubt meant to recall the British Royal Family, but it should not be confused with the Scotch Windsor *(see opposite)*. Like other whiskies made in Alberta, Windsor Canadian is exclusively rye-based.

WINDSOR CANADIAN ▶
BLENDED CANADIAN RYE 40% ABV
Honey, peaches, pine nuts, and cloves on the nose. A medium body and a sweet taste, with cereal and wood notes. An unassuming whisky; great value for money.

WISER'S

Canada

Hiram Walker Distillery, Riverside Drive East, Walkerville, Ontario
www.wisers.ca

John Philip Wiser may well have been the first distiller to use the term "Canadian Whisky" on his label, at the Chicago World's Fair in 1893. By the early 1900s, his was the third largest distillery in Canada, and its whiskies were being exported to Asia and the US.

A few years after the death of J. P. Wiser in 1917, the company was acquired by Hiram Walker. Eventually, production moved to the Hiram Walker Distillery at Walkerville. Today Wiser's are the fifth bestselling Canadian whiskies in Canada.

◀ WISER'S DELUXE
BLEND 40% ABV
A fruity and spicy nose, with cereal and linseed oil, vanilla, and toffee.

WISER'S SMALL BATCH
BLEND 43.4% ABV
This is full-flavored, with vanilla, oak, and butterscotch on the nose and in the taste. The slightly higher strength makes for more flavor and texture.

374

WOODFORD RESERVE

US

7855 McCracken Pike,
Versailles, Kentucky
www.woodfordreserve.com

Woodford Reserve is unique among bourbon distilleries in that it uses a triple distillation method and three copper pot stills for a portion of its production—the distillate comes from a column still at a separate facility also owned by Woodford Reserve. ☞

WOODFORD RESERVE DISTILLER'S SELECT ▶

BOURBON 45.2% ABV

An elegant yet robust nose, perfumed, with milk chocolate raisins, dried fruit, burned sugar, ginger, and saddle soap. Equally complex on the palate: fragrant and fruity, with raspberries, chamomile, and ginger. Lingering vanilla and peppery oak in the finish.

WOODFORD RESERVE DOUBLE OAKED

BOURBON 45.2% ABV

Oak, caramel, dark berry fruits on the nose, with orange and fudge in the background. Black pepper, vanilla, caramel, and honey on the lingering palate.

WOODFORD RESERVE

In 2005, the first bottling in the Master's Collection range was released under the Four Grain Bourbon name, and two years later a Sonoma-Cutrer Finish was added to the lineup. The Master's Collection 1838 Sweet Mash was released in 2008 to commemorate the year in which the present Woodford Reserve Distillery was constructed, and also to celebrate the historic "sweet mash" method of bourbon production.

◄ WOODFORD RESERVE MASTER'S COLLECTION 1838-STYLE WHITE CORN

BOURBON 45.2% ABV

Malt, apple, mixed nuts, and popcorn on the soft nose, while the palate yields new leather, more popcorn, spicy lemon, and pepper.

WOODFORD RESERVE STRAIGHT RYE

RYE WHISKEY 45.2% ABV

Light on the nose, with rye, black pepper, pears, and fresh oak. Rye, malt, and honey on the peppery palate, with a hint of mint.

WRITERS TEARS

Ireland

Walsh Whiskey Distillery
Royal Oak, County Carlow
www.walshwhiskey.com

Writers Tears is a pot still blended Irish whiskey produced by the Walsh family, who are also responsible for The Irishman range (*see p191*). Introduced in 2009, it contains only pot still whiskey and malt whiskey, with no grain whiskey component.

The Walsh family have recently completed a new, $34 million distillery in County Carlow. Equipped with both pot and column stills, it has the capacity to distill up to 8 million bottles of whiskey per year. The family plans to shift production of both The Irishman and Writers Tears to the distillery, with the first bottles produced there available from 2019.

WRITERS TEARS
POT STILL BLEND ▶

BLEND 40% ABV
Soft on the nose, with honey and citrus fruits. Mellow and easy-drinking, with malt, caramel, and apple notes on the long, warming palate.

A-Z OF WHISKEYS BY TYPE

Page numbers in *italics* indicate whiskey tour references.

A–Z OF WHISKEYS BY COUNTRY

Page numbers in *italics* indicate whiskey tour references.

ACKNOWLEDGMENTS

FIRST EDITION

Editor-in-Chief Charles MacLean has been writing about whiskey since 1981, and has published 15 books on the subject; *The Times* has described him as "Scotland's leading whisky expert." In 2009, he was elected Master of the Quaich (the whiskey industry's highest accolade) and, in 2012, won the "Outstanding Achievement Award" at the International Wines & Spirits Competition. Visit his website: www.whiskymax.co.uk.

Contributors: Dave Broom (Japan) • Tom Bruce-Gardyne (Scotland's malts) Ian Buxton (Scotland's blends) • Charles MacLean (Canada, Australasia, Asia) Peter Mulryan (Ireland) • Hans Offringa (Europe) • Gavin D. Smith (US).

The publishers would like to thank the following people and organizations for their help in the preparation of this book: Susan Bosanko for indexing; Robert Sharman for editing; Ann Miller at Aberlour Distillery; Rob, Robbie, and Brian at Balvenie and Glenfiddich distilleries; Dave and Heather at Bowmore Distillery; Mark and Duncan at Bruichladdich Distillery; Ewan Mackintosh at Caol Ila Distillery; Ian and Claire at Gordon & MacPhail; Ruth and Ian (Pinky) at Lagavulin Distillery; staff at the Mash Tun in Aberlour; Philip Shorten at Milroy's of Soho; The Whisky Shop Dufftown; Sukhinder Singh and staff at The Whisky Exchange, London (www.thewhiskyexchange. com); Marisa Renzullo; Casper Morris; Becky Offringa of The Whisky Couple.

Image credits: The publishers would like to thank the following producers for their assistance with this project and kind permission to reproduce their photographs in this book and related works:

Aberfeldy Distillery; Aberlour Distillery; Alberta Distillery: Alberta, Tangle Ridge, Windsor Canadian; Allied Distillers; Anchor Distilling Company: Old Potrero; Ardbeg Distillery; Bacardi & Company: Aultmore, Craigellachie, Dewar's, Royal Brackla, William Lawson's; Bakery Hill Distillery; Balcones Distilling; The Balvenie Distillery Company; Beam Global España: DYC; Beam Global Distribution (UK): The Ardmore, Laphroaig, Teacher's; Beam Global Spirits & Wine, Inc. (USA): Baker's® Kentucky Straight Bourbon Whiskey (53.5% Alc./Vol. ©CST), James B. Beam Distilling Co., Clermont, KY; Basil Hayden's® Kentucky Straight Bourbon Whiskey (40% Alc./Vol. ©CST), Kentucky Springs Distilling Co., Clermont, KY; Clermont Distillery; Jim Beam® Kentucky Straight Bourbon Whiskey (40% Alc Vol ©2009), James B. Beam Distilling Co., Clermont, KY; Kessler® American Blended Whiskey Lightweight Traveler® (40% Alc./Vol. 72.5% Grain Neutral Spirits, ©2009), Julius Kessler Company, Deerfield, IL; Knob Creek® Kentucky Straight Bourbon Whiskey (50% Alc./Vol. ©2009), Knob Creek Distillery, Clermont, KY; Maker's Mark® Bourbon Whisky (45% Alc./Vol. ©CST), Maker's Mark Distillery, Inc., Loretto, KY; Old Crow® Kentucky Straight Bourbon Whiskey (40% Alc./Vol. ©2009), W.A. Gaines, Div. of The Old Crow Distillery Company, Frankfort, KY; Old Grand-Dad® Kentucky Straight Bourbon Whiskey (43%, 50% and 57% Alc./Vol. ©2009), The Old Grand-Dad Distillery Company, Frankfort, KY; Old Taylor® Kentucky Straight Bourbon Whiskey (40% Alc./Vol. ©CST), The Old Taylor Distillery Company, Frankfort, KY; Beam Suntory: Booker's, Canadian Club, Jim Beam Devil's Cut; Benriach Distillery: Benriach, Glenglassaugh; Benrinnes Distillery; Benromach Distillery; Berry Brothers & Rudd: Cutty Sark; Betta Milk Cooperative: Hellyers Road; Bowmore Distillery; Box Distillery AB; Braunstein; Brown-Forman Corporation: Canadian Mist, Early Times, Glendronach, Old Forester, Woodford Reserve, Jack Daniel's; Bruichladdich Distillery; Bunnahabhain Distillery; Burn Stewart Distillers: Black Bottle, Deanston, Scottish Leader; The Old Bushmills Distillery Co: Bushmills, The Irishman, Knappogue Castle; Campari Drinks Group: Glen Grant, Old Smuggler, Wild Turkey 81 Proof; Cardhu Distillery; Castle Brands Inc.: Jefferson's; Chichibu Distillery: The Peated 2015; Chivas Brothers: 100 Pipers, Ballantine's, Chivas Regal, Clan Campbell, Long John, Passport, Queen Anne, Royal Salute, Something Special, Stewarts Cream of the Barley, Strathisla, Tormore; Clear Creek Distillery: McCarthy's; Clontarf Distillery; Clynelish Distillery; Compass Box Delicious Whisky; Constellation Spirits Inc.: Black Velvet®; Cooley Distillery: Connemara, Cooley, Inishowen, Kilbeggan, Locke's, Tyrconnell, Wild Geese; Corby Distilleries: Wiser's; Cragganmore Distillery; Des Menhirs: Eddu; Diageo plc: Bell's, Black & White, Buchanan's, Bulleit Bourbon, Bushmills, Caol Ila, Cardhu, Crown Royal, Dalwhinnie, Dimple, Glen Elgin, Glen Ord, Haig, J&B, Johnnie Walker, Lagavulin, Linkwood, Mortlach, Oban, Old Parr, Royal Lochnagar, Teaninich, VAT 69, White Horse, Windsor; Diageo Canada: Seagram's; Domaine Charbay: Charbay; Domaine Mavela: P&M; Echlinville Distillery: Dunville's; Edrington:

The Famous Grouse; The English Whisky Co.; The Fleischmann Distillers: Blaue Maus; Four Roses Distillery; The Gaelic Whisky Co.: Poit Dhubh; Garrison Brothers Distillery: Texas Straight Bourbon; George A. Dickel & Co.: George Dickel; Girvan Distillery; Glencadam Distillery; Glendalough Distillery; Glendullan Distillery; Glenfarclas Distillery; Glenfiddich Distillery; Glengoyne Distillery; Glengyle Distillery: Kilkerran; Glenkinchie Distillery; Glenlivet Distillery; The Glenmorangie Company: Glenmorangie, James Martin's; Glenora Distillery: Glen Breton; Glenrothes Distillery; Glenturret Distillery; Graanstokerij Filliers: Goldlys; Great Southern Distilling Company: Limeburners; Heaven Hill Distilleries, Inc.: Bernheim, Elijah Craig, Evan Williams, Heaven Hill, Georgia Moon, Mellow Corn, Old Fitzgerald, Pikesville; Highland Park Distillery; Highwood Distillers; Holle; Ian MacLeod: Langs, Tamdhu; International Beverage Holdings: anCnoc 2000, Balblair, Inver House Distillers: Hankey Bannister, Inver House, MacArthur's, Pinwinnie Royale, Speyburn; Isle of Arran: The Arran Malt, Robert Burns; John Distilleries Pvt. Ltd: Paul John; Jura Distillery; Käsers Schloss: Whisky Castle; Kentucky Bourbon Distillers, Ltd.: Johnny Drum; Kilchoman Distillery; Kirin Holdings Company: Kirin Gotemba, Kirin Karuizawa; Kittling Ridge Distillery: Forty Creek; Knockdhu Distillery: Knockeen Hills; La Maison du Whisky: Nikka; Lark Distillery: Lark Overeem Port Cask Matured; Last Drop Distillers; Loch Lomond Distillery Group: Glen Scotia; Luxco Spirited Brands: Rebel Yell; Macallan; MacDuff International: Grand Macnish, Islay Mist, Lauder's; Mackmyra; McMenamin's Group: Edgefield; Distillery: Dungourney, Green Spot, The Irishman, Midleton, Paddy, Powers, Redbreast, Tullamore D.E.W.; Morrison Bowmore Distillers: Auchentoshan, Bowmore, Glen Garioch, McClelland's, Yamazaki; Murree Distillery; The Nant Estate; New York Distilling Company: Ragtime Rye; The New Zealand Malt Whisky Company: Milford; The Nikka Whisky Distilling Co.; Chichibu, Number One Drinks Company: Chichibu, Hanyu, Ichiro's Malt; Old Pulteney Distillery; The Owl Distillery: The Belgian Owl; Pernod Ricard: Glen Keith, Miltonduff, Scapa; Pernod Ricard USA: American Spirit, Russell's Reserve, Wild Turkey; Piedmont Distillers: Catdaddy; Preiss Imports: Radico Khaitan: 8PM; Reisetbauer; Richard Joynson: Loch Fyne; Rock Town Distillery: Rock Town Arkansas Bourbon; Rogue Spirits; Rosebank Distillery; Sazerac Company, Inc.: Ancient Age, Blanton's, Buffalo Trace, Eagle Rare, Elmer T. Lee, George T. Stagg, Kentucky Gentleman®, Old Charter, Sazerac Rye, Thomas H. Handy, W.L. Weller, Very Old Barton®, Ridgemont®; Scapa Distillery; Smögen Whisky AB; Spencerfield Spirits: Pig's Nose; Speyside Distillery: Spey; Springbank Distillers: Hazelburn, Longrow, Springbank; St. George Spirits; Stock Spirits: Hammerhead; Stranahan's Colorado Whiskey; Suntory Group: Suntory Hakushu, Suntory Hibiki; Tasmania Distillery: Sullivans Cove; Teeling Distillery; Teerenpeli; Templeton Rye; Talisker Distillery; Tobermory Distillery: Ledaig, Tobermory; Tomatin Distillery: The Antiquary, Tomatin; Tomintoul Distillery; Triple Eight Distillery: The Notch; Tullibardine Distillery; Tuthilltown Distillery: Hudson; United Spirits: Signature; Us Heit Distillery: Frysk Hynder; Waldviertler Whiskydestillerie; Walsh Whiskey: Writers Tears; Wambrechies Distillery; Welsh Whisky Company: Penderyn; Wemyss Malts: Invergordon; West Cork Distillers: The Pogues; Whyte & Mackay: The Claymore, Cluny, The Dalmore, Fettercairn, Tamnavulin, Whyte & Mackay; William Grant & Sons: The Balvenie 30-year-old, Clan MacGregor, Glenfiddich, Grant's, Monkey Shoulder; Woodford Reserve Distillery: Woodford Reserve Master's Collection 1838 White Corn; Zuidam Distillery: Millstone.

Additional studio and location photography by Peter Anderson (Adnams, Armorik, Auchentoshan American Oak, Cameron Brig, Canadian Club Reserve 9-year-old, Girvan, Glen Garioch, Glenburgie, Grant's Signature, Guillon, High West, I.W. Harper, Ichiro's Malt & Grain, The Irishman Founder's Reserve, The Macallan Gold, Michter's, Rittenhouse Rye, Sam Houston, Suntory Hakushu Distiller's Reserve, Suntory Yamazaki Distiller's Reserve, Tincup, Sachin Singh (Officer's Choice), The Whisky Couple (Wild Turkey sign 230, Maker's Mark), and The Whisky Exchange (Hirsch Reserve). All other images by Thameside Media/Michael Ellis © DK Images.

Jacket images: (top row, left to right) Nikka Yoichi 10-year-old, Seagram's V.O., The Famous Grouse Mellow Gold, Redbreast 12-year-old, Kirin Gotemba Fujisanroku 18-year-old, Dimple 12-year-old, Wild Turkey 81 Proof; (bottom row, left to right) Glenfiddich 12-year-old, Old Potrero, George Dickel No.12, The Glenlivet XXV, Jameson Special Reserve 12-year-old, Jura 10-year-old, The Glenrothes 1994.

First Edition
DK INDIA Editorial Manager Glenda Fernandes **Senior Art Editor (Lead)** Navidita Thapa **DTP Manager** Sunil Sharma **Designer** Heema Sabharwal **DTP Designers** Manish Chandra Upreti, Mohammed Usman, Neeraj Bhatia
DK UK Editor Shashwati Tia Sarkar **Designer** Katherine Raj **Managing Editor** Dawn Henderson **Managing Art Editor** Marianne Markham **Senior Jacket Creative** Nicola Powling **Production Editor** Ben Marcus **Production Controller** Dominika Szczepanska **Creative Technical Support** Sonia Charbonnier